THE SEED AND THE FRUIT

THE SEED AND THE FRUIT

CHRISTIAN MORALITY IN A TIME OF TRANSITION

LESLIE STANNARD HUNTER
Bishop of Sheffield

MOREHOUSE-GORHAM CO.
NEW YORK

First published January 1953

Printed in Great Britain by
Northumberland Press Limited
Gateshead on Tyne

FOREWORD

This book contains in expanded form lectures given in September 1951 in the fine building of the faculty of Divinity of McGill University, Montreal, at the invitation of Dean James S. Thomson, who is also a native of Glasgow. The Foundation on which they were given, like the building, is the benefaction of the late W. M. Birks, of Montreal, who was a native of Ardsley—a parish in my diocese.

The subject of the lectures was of my own choosing, and I was in the first instance set to prepare a sequence of talks upon it by an invitation from the Primus of the Scottish Episcopal Church to lead a conference in Glasgow University in September 1950 on Christian Morality and the Standards of To-day, which was organized by that Church's Social Service Board and to which some Presbyterians also came. The discussions, and other discussions at conferences where I have lectured on the same subject, have enriched and enlarged my own thinking. In the footnotes and by quotation I have indicated some of the more recent writers to which I am obviously indebted.

The essay on Eternal Life, in its original form, was printed a good many years ago in *The Pilgrim*, that short-lived quarterly which Archbishop Temple once edited, and I am obliged to Messrs. Longman and Co. for permission to reproduce it.

L.S.

Sheffield
November, 1951

CONTENTS

As the threats of war and the cries of the dispossessed were sounding in his ears, Western Man fell into an uneasy sleep. In his sleep he dreamed that he entered the spacious store in which the gifts of God to men are kept, and addressed the angel behind the counter, saying: 'I have run out of the fruits of the Spirit. Can you restock me?' When the angel seemed about to say no, he burst out, 'In place of war, afflictions, injustice, lying and lust, I need love, joy, peace, integrity, discipline. Without these I shall be lost.' And the angel behind the counter replied, 'We do not stock fruits, only seeds.'

I

INTRODUCTION:

ARE MORAL STANDARDS DECLINING?

TWENTY years ago Bishop Barry began his book on *The Relevance of Christianity* with this sentence: 'Incomparably the most imperious challenge which to-day confronts Christianity is the moral chaos of our generation.' Only a stout optimist would affirm that the moral standards of 1951 were an improvement on those of 1931. It is very generally assumed in ecclesiastical circles that there has been a slump in morals, especially since 1939. Nevertheless, we may get away on the wrong foot if we start by accepting without question the assumption that moral standards have deteriorated since some unspecified date and if we do not look for evidence which may point the other way. It is necessary, for one thing, to take a longer span than just the period since 1939, before the comparison becomes illuminating.

Though people often compare one decade or generation with another, it is in truth not easy to support with accurate evidence the assertion that this was better or worse than that. We ourselves are changing all the time, and our objective judgments are often oddly and humorously subjective. As we get on in years we have a nostalgia for 'the good old times', unmindful that kindly memory often allows us to forget the darker shadows; we are apt to speak of 'young people nowadays' in a tone which implies that they are not what young people once were. Again, it is easy to focus upon a particular set of facts and fail to look at the general pattern of society, and to argue from the conditions of one class or group as though it were the whole of society.

How far is the judgment that morals have deteriorated a fair overall diagnosis of British society?

In its favour are many facts that are painfully familiar. There has been a great increase in the number of divorces and broken homes, and probably in sexual promiscuity. In England and Wales, the year 1937 saw 5,903 divorce petitions filed, 5,195 decrees nisi of dissolution or nullity pronounced and 4,886 decrees made absolute. In 1947, 48,501 petitions were filed, 53,792 decrees nisi were pronounced, 60,190 decrees were made absolute.[1] A ten-fold increase in decrees nisi and eight-fold increase in petitions filed are disquieting figures even when one has made allowance for the abnormal conditions caused by a long war. Not less disquieting is the number of children conceived outside marriage—in 1947 the figure was one in every eight in England and Wales, and of these the illegitimates were one in eighteen (an improvement on 1945 when the ratio was nearly 1/10th).

Then there has been a great increase in juvenile delinquency, pilfering and robbery with violence, consequent upon two wars, a decline in parental control and a shortage of policemen on the beat. The number of known robberies with violence in 1937 was 209, in 1947 979, and in 1949 990.[2]

It is commonly asserted that in commerce business standards are not what they were, that the sense of obligation and responsibility has declined and that there is less honest work and more absenteeism. Gambling and betting have increased, and there is more drinking

[1] Cf. Marriage Guidance Bulletin, January 1950.

[2] Return given by Lord Chancellor in the House of Lords, April 18th, 1950.

though less drunkenness.[3] Gambling and betting have become the major social evil of our time. The habit has extended to women and children. Whereas there is a good deal of evidence of people spending far beyond their means on this amusement, and of many broken homes being one of its consequences, the problem which confronts moralists and all who care for social welfare and culture is the immense amount of money and time expended in gambling and betting for small sums—and the continual pressure on men and women in works and factories to do it.

There is also spreading from Hollywood, in sharp contrast to Puritan ideals, the view that happiness is the chief end to pursue in life, and therefore that the fulfilment of desire should determine a man's choices and conduct. In a land of plenty, hedonism can easily become a man's actual religion, whatever he may profess. In Britain, also, some would even go so far as to say that 'Why shouldn't I?' has taken the place of the Ten Commandments for a great many people. Finally, there is some ground for anxiety lest the development of social security and state paternalism may eventually cause a loss of initiative and of the sense of obligation, and may even make people pusillanimous. (It is to correct this tendency that the well-conceived schools of the 'Outward Bound'[4] movement have been started.)

How, for example, are we to judge the way in which young men and women plunge into matrimony long before they are in a position 'to set up a home', to use a phrase of former times? The facts cannot be gain-

[3] It is to be noted, however, that since 1946 there has been an increase in the proved cases of drunkenness—the increase in 1950 over 1949 being no less than 33 per cent in England and Wales. This may be partly due to more activity on the part of the police.

[4] Information about the Outward Bound schools and their aims may be obtained from the Secretary of the Outward Bound Trust, 40 Broadway, London, S.W.1.

said. The poor have always married young as a result of economic pressures. The wage of an unskilled labourer used to reach maximum soon after he had reached twenty. Overcrowded houses encouraged him to move out and set up on his own. These circumstances also tended towards early courtship and to some extent towards sexual relations before marriage. The middle and professional classes were not in times past subject to these pressures. Even a generation ago, it would have been thought lax and decadent for a young pair to marry before the man could support a wife and family, even frugally. It was also thought right that a man should complete his training and begin his job before he contemplated matrimony, and that it was not asking the impossible of him to control his biological and sexual urges for a good many years. To-day, however, partly in consequence of the fact that the sexes mix much more freely and fully from school-time onwards, students get married while they are entirely dependent on public grants. One immediate consequence is that the man is limited in his range of choice of a job, while for some years it may not be possible for the couple to have a home of their own or to start having a family. As far as the Christian ministry is concerned, these early marriages usually prevent a man from offering himself freely to serve God and the Church wherever he may be most serviceable. In consequence there is a good deal of humbug thought and talked about vocation, which makes a bad beginning for the full commitment that the modern situation demands of the ordained ministry of the Church.

In view of these facts, and some more like them, it is not unreasonable to take a pessimistic view of present-day morals, especially when you take into account the state of international politics. The catastrophic decline in active church membership since the beginning of the century has also to be taken into account. There is now growing up the third generation of people who have had no effective contact with the churches and their teaching —people who are not hostile to the doctrines and principles of the Christian faith, but are ignorant of them and therefore do not recognize their authority.

It is a temptation for good church people who see the contemporary picture like this to take fright, and even, God forgive 'em, to thank God that they at least are not as these other abandoned folk are: or to adopt an attitude similar to that of some ecclesiastics towards Church Reform—'Let be; it will last my time'. Like other temptations, these have to be resisted and overcome. Resistance will be strengthened by a consideration of present-day trends at a deeper level, for it may show that this nervously depressing picture is not the whole truth.

I

The outstanding fact about society to-day is not deterioration, but the fact that the *pattern of society* has been changing. It is changing largely as a result of political influences, economic pressures and technical advances.

Until a few years ago the incentives to work in industrial society were, on the one hand, fear of unemployment and of poverty, and, on the other, greed and acquisitiveness, which had their rewards. A society which has achieved full employment and security and in which there is comparatively little poverty asks of men and women moral qualities which the former order of things did not call out. It also brings new temptations which they are not trained to resist. The industrial worker for five or six generations until quite recently had been made irresponsible by the conditions of employment. He or she was just 'a hand' who could be stood off at short notice, and very badly paid at that. It takes a long time to work an evil such as this out of society's system. Only slowly will a new order that gives a man security for insecurity and asks of him responsibility instead of irresponsibility get the response for which it asks.

Ordinary folk in their opinions and conduct are imitative rather than original and creative.[5] They are 'conditioned' by the society in which they live far more than they realize, and not least by the economic pressures existing in it. One illustration of this is the way in which people who will live decent, law-abiding lives in a stable, orderly society may be thrown clean off their balance if that society is violently disrupted. During the past twenty years, in some countries more than others, society has become violently disrupted, normal family life has broken up, living conditions have deteriorated, and so forth. In European countries where famine conditions have obtained, many people have been tempted to steal and to take advantage of neighbours, who would never have felt the slightest temptation so to do in former days. Homeless refugees and displaced persons have been forced to live by a new scale of values and priorities. A good deal of the sexual laxity and delinquency that exist in Europe is due to human beings having to live under conditions under which God never willed that they should live, and who in consequence are tempted beyond their strength. To a lesser degree, similar pressures have had similar effects in Great Britain. There are grounds for hoping that the alarming figures for juvenile delinquency and broken marriages may diminish as we get further away from the war.

We have also to recognize, more than Christians of

[5] Cf. Arnold Toynbee, *A Study of History*, abridged edition, pp. 213-16.

last century did, that individual conduct and moral judgment are powerfully influenced, if not determined, by economic pressures in industrial society. If these pressures are making some people irresponsible in regard to their work or greedy in regard to their remuneration, or over-anxious in regard to their security or over-crowded in their homes, it is not sufficient that the Church should say to individuals, 'Don't be irresponsible, don't covet, be not anxious, be disciplined in matters of sex, honour your father and mother', it has to recognize that these pressures are stronger than they should be. It ought therefore to enlist its members in an attack upon all such hindrances to the good life.[6]

Along with this, let us also recognize that in some respects moral standards have greatly improved. There is more general acceptance of social obligations. To take a small example, people in this country are much more disciplined in 'taking their turn', standing patiently in queues and accepting 'fair shares' than they used to be or than people are in some other countries. The individualism of the middle classes has been infiltrated by the much stronger social sense of the poor. At the same time, the crudity and cruelties of life among the very poor a century ago have given place to a more civilized and humane standard of life. Again, a hundred years ago in this country, in cities like Glasgow and Sheffield, at the peak of church-going, large numbers of families who were the cannon fodder of industry lived like animals, bred like animals, died like animals, and industrialists and their wives and families who attended church on the Sabbath were content to have it so![7] To-day even the lowest ranks of industrial workers are living on a different level altogether of health, culture,

[6] Unfortunately the Church has tended to leave this to others and to concentrate on ambulance work.

[7] Cf. John Hunter, *A Life*, pp. 121-3.

social habit, decency. The change for the better has been immense. At the other end of the scale, if I may put it so, the modern industrialist is a much more moral being than his grandfather. Willy nilly, he accepts a social responsibility towards his employees and towards society; he treats them, he has to treat them, as human beings with rights and liberties. In the last years he has had to exercise real care of the juveniles that he employs —partly no doubt because there are fewer juveniles to employ, and therefore industry can no longer afford to waste the country's youth as it used to do. This is not just physical betterment, it is moral betterment. In many of the best organized industries, there is a genuine concern for the welfare of the employee which has brought into existence a new profession, the Personnel Manager, while for a long time now the state's factory inspectors have brought about no small revolution in working conditions and factory hygiene, and have promoted a steady flow of wise social legislation. In addition, the comradeship in service of two world wars, and especially perhaps of the civil defence services during the last war, have broken down class barriers and the suspicions and distrust which they create.

Early in 1940, Sir Wyndham Deedes, that fine Englishman, stayed with me for a night after he had come back from a visit to Turkey, a country he knew intimately. He expressed concern as to the moral fibre of the younger generation in our country: they seemed to him to compare unfavourably with the young Turks. A few months later came the time of testing for the people of our land, and how splendidly they rose to the occasion; how fine the comradeship, the devotion to duty, the quiet steady acceptance of danger, hardship and short rations!

At the present time while some of the propertied classes moon and moan about moral decadence and falling standards, the so-called working-classes are conscious of great progress in social betterment. They are better fed, they are free of haunting and depressing insecurities: many of them are well-housed. Their religion may be sketchy, but their moral standards are better than their beliefs, and their domestic practice better than those portrayed in the amusements which the vested interests in their amusements provide. Corporately, they may laugh at the wrong things, but in their private life their moral judgment is pretty sound. The facts and figures of broken marriages, disquieting though they be, have to be set against the general acceptance of woman as a *persona*, and no longer just the chattel of the male. There is more real comradeship between man and wife, boy and girl, a deal less cruelty and unhappiness in the home to-day than a hundred years ago. And in spite of all that can be truly said about parental irresponsibility, there is a more widespread sense of responsibility in the bringing of children into the world, and more care for them when they come. The changes in industrial society of recent years have not all been for the worse. Whole areas of life which religious men a century ago assumed to be outside the moral law are now recognized to come within its sway. (E.g. the attitude 'Business is business and religion is religion, and I don't let them mix' is now discredited.) Churchmen have to be on their guard against over-simplifying moral issues, and dealing with them in isolation from their political, social and economic setting. Nevertheless, a time when society is on the move, when powerful commercial interests are corrupting the tastes and standards of the people, when the little man, confronted by great concentrations of power and by a universe limitless in time and space, feels helpless and small, is a time for watchfulness. Individual Christians and the Christian community ought to be active and creative. Our concern should be directed not so much to possible declines in morality as to the more evident decline in men's faith in God and belief in eternal life, and the consequent weakening of their belief in a moral law which men and nations must obey, because it is not of man's making but of God's.

What is certain about the present situation is that principles and conventions that have been accepted as Christian principles and practices are no longer generally accepted. As I have said, for three or four generations now the younger generation, by and large, has been out of touch with church teaching. We are no longer living in a static society which took a great deal for granted in the spheres of religion and morals. It is undoubtedly a testimony to the strength of the Christian tradition among the British people that a society so remiss in its religious practices and so vague and uncertain in its theological beliefs should continue to believe in the distinctions between right and wrong, truth and falsehood, good and evil, and should maintain a moderately good moral tone. But it is a precarious situation which no believer or moralist will view with complacency, for it might lead into a moral decline and rot unless society recovers a faith and a belief which win acceptance both in school and university and in the places where the workers gather.

II

It is when we look beyond personal conduct and domestic relationships to the wider field of politics and try to estimate the influence of political institutions in the modern world upon the life of individuals that there is indeed cause for disquiet. In no country as yet have men succeeded in achieving both freedom and social justice. The culture of Greece, of Western Europe in the thirteenth century, of the Renaissance, rested upon slave-labour. The political freedom of England in the Victorian era and the rapid expansion of its wealth went with the economic servitude of the many. For the first time in history, the attempt is now being made to achieve both justice and freedom throughout a whole society and also to maintain a fair standard of life. Within the historic process it may not be possible to achieve this synthesis and union fully, but society presses on—moved both by the conscience of those who have and by the agitation of the 'have nots'. The immense effort in a country such as ours to give a fairer deal to the under-privileged and the under-paid manual workers has brought into being the vast army of civil servants and functionaries of the welfare state. People are being regimented as they have never been before. Is it just bad luck or an ominous sign that the first casualty in the construction of an educational ladder, giving to poor as well as rich the benefits of higher education, should be the free grammar school, and the second the subordination of the headmaster to the educational administrator? What is clear is that politics and economics cannot of themselves achieve a society which is at the same time both just and free. Again, what has been called technocracy weights the scales in favour of the impersonal state (and the large-scale industrial unit) against the individual and the family. Socialism as well as Capitalism might quite easily destroy the freedom of the little man as Communism does. It would be a sad progress if the industrial 'hand' ended up as the human robot in a totalitarian state with no mind to call his own and no will to think freely or act creatively.

If these things happen in the green tree in which the sap of freedom has been vigorous for centuries as a result of Christian traditions, what are we to think of the countries where the creed of the rulers is the Marxian philosophy with its sharp denial of the Christian faith and where manners are cruel and torture of a devilish kind is part of the normal machinery of government? The fact that such a tyranny should have imposed itself upon Eastern Europe and much of Asia and should have some followers and fellow-travellers among the scientific humanists, technicians and the manual workers, including some muddle-headed Christians, in every country of the world, is a judgment of God upon the failure of countries that value freedom to achieve social justice, and upon the failure of the Christian Church in them to achieve a prophetic witness through its corporate life. Nevertheless, since God is love, His judgments are not unto despair, but unto repentance and hope. While history runs its course, it is never too late to change the trends of social behaviour and political action.

The crisis of our political failure has come because somehow or other Christians have allowed the policies of 'Christendom' to be both formulated and executed without regard to the eternal verities. Utopianism has been allowed to take the place of the Kingdom of God. Men have been allowed to think that they can live the good life in community while they forget their sonship to God and their urgent need of redemption and grace before they can live as brethren. The tension between social justice and freedom, between democracy and the rights of the individual as a child of God, can never be completely resolved in history. They will only be held without breaking and conflict in a society where men are one in the acceptance of the Christian doctrine of sin and of grace, and in humble duty to the Eternal God. It is important that Christians, especially those who are to teach the faith, should get their minds clear on this point. There are no grounds in Christian revelation or in Christian experience for expecting that a change in political order and economic system, any more than psychology in the class-room, will eradicate the evil in human nature. The relevant word to our condition that speaks out of the life and teaching of our Lord, is saying, Yes, believe in the essential goodness of men and women as He did: persevere with all the help the sciences can give in removing the hindrances to the good life in society, and in increasing industrial efficiency, change if needs be its pattern, so as to give that essential goodness air to breathe, room to grow and bear fruit. But when you have done all that, do not think you have done more than that. And as to new techniques, while they greatly enrich life and put new powers and tools in the ordinary man's grasp, do not forget that they still leave him with himself to deal with. There remains deep-set in human personality, pride, selfishness and a terrible inertia. These proceed from within. Again and again, they spoil human relationships, break up the working-team, slow up the day's work, prevent the best of programmes from being carried through. The power to control and overcome these lies outside the laboratory and the consulting-room, and beyond planning and politics, in the realm of the spirit where God speaks to men with creative power. 'Thy sins are forgiven thee: go, sin no more.' 'I came that they might have life.'

In the sphere of secular politics, even the best men can only do what is best in circumstances and situations which they cannot fully control. Their action will only be relatively right, rarely absolutely so. The statesman, the Trade Union leader, the business executive, who have to represent a body of people, some of whom are professing Christians, many of whom are not, are always confronted with this tension. This does not excuse them for taking the line of least resistance and lapsing into cynicism. Each in his station has to take his courage in his hands, to lead as well as represent, and having done the best he can, to say, God be merciful to me, a sinner.

Christian idealists who claim the authority of the

Gospel for their political programmes in an evil world are guilty of confusing political relativity with the absolutes of religion. Their muddle-headedness lays them open to the attack of the critics of the Faith, and weakens the effectiveness of the Christian Church in the world. Reinhold Niebuhr has dealt with this subject with such penetration that I would only add this rider. The genius of British politics has lain precisely in its empiricism. It contrasts with—and vastly annoys—the theoretical ideologist; but its fruits have been appreciable while those of the ideologist and idealist only too often are sour grapes or dead-sea fruits. This empirical approach still remains the great contribution which the democracies of the Commonwealth have to contribute to world affairs.

II

MORALITY AND CHRISTIAN MORALITY

In Western society, Law and Morals for the past thousand years have rested on and been moulded by the Christian doctrines of God and man and of eternal life. That is not to say that Western society has been thoroughly Christian in its culture and morals. But it has been more Christian than anything else.[1] The administration of Justice, for example, rests on the Ten Commandments; while the accepted view of the family is that of Christian monogamy. At the same time that Law and Morality have had these theological roots, they have also in their values and priorities reflected the social order in every age; and there have been long periods—feudalism for example—when the social pattern remained almost unchanged. In sharp contrast with these long, static periods of history, we are living in a period of rapid and drastic change—in some countries, revolutionary, in others like our own, evolutionary. A period of social change confronts the Church with moral problems and challenges, partly because its ethical teaching in the static period prior to the time of unsettlement has been closely related to the political and social structure. When that structure begins to give way the hold of the ethical principles also becomes shaky. For example, the motive for honesty in the age we have left behind was closely tied to the rights of property. Two world wars have greatly weakened popular belief in the rights of property.

[1] T. S. Eliot, *The Idea of a Christian Society*, p. 13.

Consequently, people have become much less honest and will continue to be less honest until a motive and incentive for honesty are found which tie into the pattern of a new society—a society that is not likely to regard property as the Georgians and Victorians did.

The moral principles which are proclaimed by Christians as the moral law of God are simply and shortly stated. Those of the Ten Commandments which concern human relationships are based on the belief that the family and the state are divinely ordained for the welfare of man. Justice is recognized to be the basic principle of social order because the individual is a potential child of God and inheritor of eternal life and must therefore be treated as a person worthy of honour and respect. The Church has a duty to impress upon people, not least politicians and scientists, the degree to which the rights and liberties of man rest upon the belief that he is the child of a merciful and just God and an inheritor of eternal life. If belief in the worth of every human being ceased to be the bedrock of social morality, then it would be much harder to resist the over-riding claims of the totalitarian state, or the kind of totalitarian arguments put forward in favour of the sterilization of mental defectives or the liquidation of incurables.[2]

[2] 'I respect every man according to his worth,' said Lucian. 'I trust you are not going to reproach me on that score.'

'You respect man just as you would respect a car, in proportion to its precise market value.'

'What's wrong with that?' asked Lucian.

'. . . What I want to know is whether you respect man as such, as of value to himself, unique and irreplaceable, even when the individual has not utility value, and when he arouses neither your pity nor your love for him as an animal.'

'I have never asked myself that question,' said Lucian. 'I know that I respect a man in proportion to his social value and as a living animal. Everybody thinks and feels the way I do. . . . It is the only logical conclusion. Man is a unit of social value. Every-

These principles on which morality is founded can be written out on a sheet of notepaper. Granted the principles, the tough business is to apply them in concrete situations, especially the concrete situations that arise in an imperfect world in which the choices are not always clearly between good and evil, but often between two goods or two evils, greater or lesser. For a Christian, many of the most acute moral problems are due to the tension between what Lord Lindsay has described 'as the morality of my station and my duties and the challenge of perfection or the morality of grace'. For a Christian, moral conduct depends on right choices which in turn derive from true insights. Therefore I would venture to define morality as *the wisdom of human intercourse,* adding as a rider that the fear of the Lord is the beginning of such wisdom.

Let us pause on those two words, *intercourse* and

thing else is pure hypothesis.' *The 25th Hour,* by Virgil Gheorghiu, pp. 136-7.

The conversation, which contains the theme of this powerful and painful story, concludes with the assertion of the father of Lucian, who is a statesman of the pre-totalitarian school—'The emergence of a Technological Civilization has meanwhile destroyed what we had achieved and won through centuries of civilization. Technological Civilization has re-introduced human sacrifice and the disregard for Man. To-day, Man is reduced to the single dimension of his social value.'

A similar thought and fear runs through *Return from Utopia,* by Richard Law, the conservative politician. It ends with a powerful plea for a return to Christianity. See especially pp. 180-1 and to end. 'To-day . . . there are plenty to affirm that political liberty is a meaningless abstraction unless it is combined with economic security; that human personality is a myth or a chemical formula; and that man signifies nothing except a digit, a social unit, a cog in a vast and impersonal machine. In little more than a generation there has been a revolution of ideas more far-reaching and more terrible than the world has known for 500 years, perhaps more terrible than anything it has ever known. It is terrible because it threatens the very existence of man.' Cf. also Karl Stern, *The Pillar of Fire,* quoted on p. 60.

human. In a different context, Professor John Baillie says, 'Neither an organism nor anything else can grow in any other way than by taking up into itself from that which surrounds it. Hence no being could grow if it were surrounded by nothing.'[3] Or, to use a phrase that has became current, All life is meeting. Human relationships can be crude and barbarous, or they may be wholesome and lovely: but relationships there must be. The good God has so decreed it. Therefore the wise man and the wise community will try to find out the why and wherefore of God's creative purpose and to order all the relationships of life in such a way as to conform with, and to implement, that purpose.

Human beings have relationships of many kinds, one with another, individually and in families and in other social groups. Because men are endowed with powers of remembering and reflecting, of reasoning and of hoping, these relationships take on a pattern and have a complexity quite other than the simple instinctive relationships of the animals. While meeting is a sheer fact of life and is an end and a joy in itself, human intercourse and community life cannot just be left to happen and to be guided by instinct. Neither can they be ordered by rule of thumb. They have to be ruled by reason. As I have said, the rules or principles may be few, it is their expression in concrete situations and particular relationships that requires most thought. Consequently, insight and wisdom have a large place in morality and moral conduct. Significantly, it is the wisdom literature of the Bible that is largely concerned with morality, and the relationships of daily life. The wisdom of human intercourse brings together the knowledge of first principles and experience of life in such a way as to perfect men in the art and the science of living together.

The good life is a way of living on the part of in-

[3] John Baillie, *The Belief in Progress*, p. 161.

dividuals and groups, which will bring to the whole community the fullest measure of those qualities and fruits which make life of most worth. The answer to the question, what is best for me to do in this situation, cannot be answered truly if a man were only to do what is right in his own eyes or to estimate the good only in terms of what was to his own soul's health. While the growth to full personality of an individual here and hereafter is a true end, it is not the only end for him in life.

The relationships of home, community, nation or Church, are not only means by which the individual may grow in wisdom and grace, and be schooled for the life of the world to come. They have a significance of their own and are the objects of God's redemptive purpose. When the Church's teaching has concentrated too exclusively on the salvation of the individual he has been encouraged to think that so long as he reaches the haven where he would be, the fate of other souls and of the society to which he belongs need not be his serious concern. Professor Quick in the lectures published after his death shows that the Church in the Middle Ages under the influence of Greek and Latin thought moved away from the emphasis on the cosmic significance of Christ's death and resurrection to an emphasis on individual salvation. 'The destiny of the individual soul and its determination at the hour of death, not the regeneration and restoration of all things . . . come to hold the central place. . . .'[4] It was this undue emphasis in the nineteenth century evangelicalism which led many thinkers and men of action to turn away from Christianity as they understood it, and to set their hopes upon a doctrine of progress and development of human society in this life, and to devote themselves passionately to the cause of social justice and to the increase of knowledge,

[4] Quick, *The Gospel of the New World*, Ch. 5.

believing that in doing this they were interpreting truly the mind of God revealed in Jesus Christ.

It does not fall within the scope of these addresses to discuss how far the belief in progress which has taken so strong a hold upon Christians and non-Christians alike in the Western world is a reasonable belief. The subject has been fully and critically discussed in Professor John Baillie's, *The Belief in Progress.*[5] My purpose in mentioning it now is only to insist that Christian morality requires us to think not only of the welfare of the individual, but also of the family and of the community, and of good relations between communities. The good life is that which is best both for me and my neighbours, for individual and community. There may often be tension between what seems the highest good for the individual and what seems best for other individuals and for the community as a whole. But we must assume that always and everywhere the individual achieves the good life in and through the service and building up of the community of which he is a member. Therefore, *one* criterion of what is right and what is wrong for men to think or do is whether the particular thought, judgment or action will contribute to the greatest good of the greatest number. Such a standard can only be a very rough and ready one, but it has universal validity like a law of physics. The rightness of any human action is not to be judged solely by the conscience and the purity of motive of the actor, but also by its consequences, and not least by its influence on the welfare of the community within which he lives. And further, we must not allow ourselves to draw the limits of that community

[5] The Christian belief is no easy optimism that the world is getting better and better every century or that man can build Jerusalem in England's green and pleasant land or anywhere else by his own efforts. The New Testament has no sure belief in progress apart from the creative Spirit and from Him whom it acclaims as the Way, the Truth and the Life.

too narrowly. Each of us belongs to more than one community—and no one of these can claim our total loyalty—family, neighbourhood, profession or industry, nation, the community of nations, Church; to each and all must heed be given.

Part of the Church's problem is that society, in moving away from the crude individualism of eighteenth and nineteenth century industrialism, has also rejected its Puritan ethic. The Puritans, who had a long innings in Scotland and have left many vestigial traces in the thought and practice of the British Commonwealth, like the Pharisees, tried to reduce the good life to a set of rules and to stretch the coverlet of morality to cover the whole of life. Many of my generation or older, if they recollect their childhood, will remember that the God to whom they were introduced by parents and teachers was One who was only or chiefly interested in conduct and was always watching how they were behaving. The climax of the nursery prayer was, 'Forgive me for being a bad boy, help me to be a good boy'. But there are whole tracts of a child's life—and very innocent and happy going—from which a God who is only interested in good conduct is shut out. In this the child is father of the man. There are also large tracts of our adult life into which issues of right and wrong do not intrude. The appreciation of beauty, scientific discovery, technical skill and precision, much business, much meeting, are experiences which cannot be reduced to the black and white of moral decision without being spoilt, stunted and emptied of their rich context. It has been this attempt to identify religion with morality that has often made worship a difficult and joyless thing.

The Christian way of life as taught and exemplified by the Lord Jesus, was a way of life which followed from the belief that man was capable of communion with the everlasting God and was therefore made—not for a brief inconclusive, partial growth in god-likeness, but to grow through the action of the Holy Spirit upon his spirit into life eternal. While our Lord speaks of the Kingdom of God and of Eternal Life in a way which sometimes leaves one in doubt whether He is speaking of a life within man's compass here and now, or of the fruition of communion with God in eternity, while much of His ethical teaching has a vivid concreteness and close application to a particular setting, His mind all the time is fixed on the end and fruition of life, when the will of God is perfectly obeyed and love makes full and glad response to love. St. Paul also relates his moral exhortations closely to the fact of resurrection unto eternal life.

> 'If ye be risen with Christ seek those things which are above . . . mortify therefore your members which are upon earth . . . put on bowels of mercies, kindness, humbleness of mind, meekness, long-suffering, forbearing one another, and forgiving one another . . . and above all these put on charity which is the bond of perfectness.' (Colossians, ch. 3.)

It would be difficult to get sanction for so strenuous a moral and spiritual demand if man's citizenship were confined to the imperfect politics of this world, and if his growth ended after a few decades of adult life.

That being true, how disastrous for social morality is the loss of an operative faith in eternal life in the modern world, even among professing Christians! How important that Christian teachers, undismayed by the little we can say or imagine about the nature of the future life, should bend their abilities to making belief in eternal life a genuine intellectual option and a faith governing men's moral decisions and judgments of value here and now! The best efforts of the ordained ministry of the Church should be directed to making the teaching in pulpit and class concerning eternal life, especially from Easter to Whit Sunday, cogent and closely related to the business of daily life, eschewing both an over-emphatic dogmatism about things which cannot be proved and a vague and escapist sentimentalism.[6]

(In parenthesis, may I make this personal confession? The perplexity about the nature of eternal life which worries me is not the problem of quantity, of meeting again and all that, which is so completely beyond our imagining that we can only leave it to God and reverently hope for the best. My own perplexity is this. Much of the little in me which seems to have the quality of eternity and which seems least in need of purification and reform, is the power to be in harmony with and to enjoy earth and water, wood and rock—the stuff of this earth which we apprehend through our senses. These and I are of the same stuff. In the infinite variety of shape, colour and fragrance which there is upon this globe, and which far exceeds in wonder and beauty all the works of man, both pious and secular—in these shapes, colours and fragrances of the natural world, my whole being rejoices. Life without them and the means of appreciating them would be an impoverished life; and when to this is added our kinship with and love of the beasts that perish—one's perplexity in regard to eternal life deepens. Frankly, the unending discussions of a theological Senior Common Room, with angels making soft music off-scene would be no replacement. Philosophers may be satisfied with abstractions, but the ordinary man, like the poet, desires the concrete things which make the natural world, where no two scenes are alike, so entrancing and satisfying.)

Even if it alarms some of our fellow-citizens we have to set before society a conception of the good life, whole,

[6] Cf. Ch. VI, *infra*.

many-sided, sacramental, as an alternative to Puritanism—and not less robust. We may appear to the Puritan or to the mere moralist to be giving away a lot of positions, but it has to be done in the name of truth. The root of the matter is to persuade men to accept *obligation* as *the* motive in life. I am under obligation to think of my neighbour, all my neighbours, all my fellow-men as people like myself, to be treated as I would treat myself. This is the rational basis for sexual continence and fidelity in marriage; for doing a day's work; for keeping promises, for being honest, for the acceptance of responsibility, for resisting the attraction of money. It is the price of freedom in a free democracy. The cost to the individual or to one single group in the community may be high. It will demand training, discipline, self-mastery, sacrifice. A proof that this is the true way of life is the harmony and satisfaction that it brings to the individual, and the peace and fellowship that it brings to a community—even joy in the act of sacrifice.

I refrain from stealing my neighbour's purse or breaking into his house because I respect his person and have an obligation not to injure him. If he has more possessions than is good for him or can be squared with social justice, it is not for another individual to lighten his load, for that, like lynching, would lead to anarchy and humbug, but for the community to take appropriate action. Can you see any sufficient dynamic for social righteousness in a democratic, free society other than this sense of obligation, freely accepted, by individuals towards one another and towards the community, and by communities towards other communities—a universal lease-lend, if you like? If that is so, then a good deal of the moral exposition put out in the name of the Church misses the mark because it is shaped to the pattern of a society that is past or passing—the feudal hierarchy, or *laissez-faire* capitalism, or times when production and supply fell far short of need and men lived on the margin of famine.

If in a time of full employment and minimum wages a man has a quite uninteresting job, what other incentive can he have to keep going steadily day in day out, but a sense of obligation to his work-mates and to the industrial society of which he is a part? As I pointed out in my first talk, ordinary folk are imitative rather than creative; therefore their sense of obligation can be strengthened by the ordering of society. Just as totalitarianism or *laissez-faire* capitalism or too much state paternalism weakens the sense of obligation, so in a society more Christian in its pattern it could be elicited and strengthened.[7]

The sense of obligation is intensified and becomes more powerful when it takes the more personal form of loyalty. This may happen under the pressure of an emergency. How else can one explain the superb gallantry shown by rescuers in a pit disaster, or by many civilians during air raids, who had not the discipline under fire which is inculcated by military training and upheld by comradeship in arms?

Obligation is most completely sublimated when it becomes disinterested love issuing in sacrifice. Then indeed all things are possible. Christians knowing their own selfish and sinful hearts, rightly doubt whether that fine moral quality of life can be sustained in ordinary people without the dynamic of religious faith, and precisely a faith that the Word of God, the mystery of creation, became clear in the Incarnation and Death of

[7] Idealists and reformers neglect at peril the fact of human sin, pride and self-interest. They ought always to ask, What is best in existing circumstances and taking into account the weaknesses of human nature. *Pace* Nye Bevan, it may be better for the individual as well as for the finances of the country that he should pay a proportion of the cost of his dentures and spectacles.

Jesus—the act of God in history—an act of pure, disinterested love.

Therefore the continuous task of the Church, and a first priority in its ministry, must be to revive and sustain an operative faith in the living God, who once and for all revealed certain moral absolutes in the living and dying of Jesus Christ, and in whom every new generation has to live and move and find the dynamic of its being. In the end, all our ethical and pastoral problems lead us back to this evangelistic task, but, I believe, that in our time, the task will not be discharged by a multiplication of preachments and of teachers, but rather by a demonstration on the part of the whole church community of more Christian living—the morality of grace.

III

THE MORALITY OF GRACE

'THE WAY' is the oldest of the names by which the religion of Jesus has been known. It was the way of life of the early Christian communities that captured the heart of the world in which they were set. Men not only heard about the Cross and the Resurrection from its preachers, they saw the Cross and the power of the Cross in their lives. And they marvelled.

This way of life was a life of faith. Jesus, our Lord, substituted love for fear as the dominant motive in life because the God whom He declared unto men was the Great Lover. The life of the community which He sketched with a few broad strokes was 'the Kingdom of God': its ideal no less than 'be ye perfect even as your heavenly Father is perfect': the motive for generosity and forgiveness, 'that ye may be sons of your Father who is in heaven, for He maketh His sun to rise on the evil and the good, and sendeth rain on the just and the unjust'. Men and women were not told to love one another in order to solve the social problem and prevent war, but because they cannot love God truly unless they do love and care about their brother-man. The religion and the ethic are one seamless robe, as the first epistle of St. John reiterates. Again and again, that writer brings out the religious derivation of the morality and the moral consequences of the religion—'He that hath the Son hath life, and he that hath not the Son hath not the life'.

This morality of grace was in sharp contrast with the

legal morality of the Pharisees. A legal morality tends to identify goodness with blamelessness and to appeal chiefly to the motive of fear—the fear of making a mistake and of failure, which makes men afraid to take risks. In practice, the burden which it laid on common folk was not only the tiresome burden of a lot of rules and regulations, but also a besetting fear, lest having kept them, there might be some other good work to be done before they would merit their reward. The Pharisees and the Puritans after them caricatured the best moral teaching in the Old Testament, which has permanent validity. The morality of the Old Testament on the whole is a prudential, commonsense morality of one's station and duties in the world, in which is mirrored the conception of God as Law-giver and Magistrate. There is, indeed, a prudence which is as unselfish as some kinds of venturesomeness are a public nuisance. 'Look before you leap,' 'Safety first' are not always selfish counsels. Although our Lord chose as apostles men, with fire in their bellies, he expected them to consume their smoke and count in advance the cost of their enterprises. Neither did He despise the sound, steady, level-headed type of character which the Old Testament ethic moulded.

None the less, the element in faith on which He laid most stress, as Oliver Quick once said in a sermon, was 'not trustworthiness but trustfulness'. In the parables of commerce, it is upon the element of adventure, of acting promptly and of taking risks, that He fastens. It is not that He approved of unrighteous stewards or gamblers, but that in His judgment religious people were often so afraid that their light would blow out or that the treasure given them would be stolen that they hid the light so that it could not be seen, and buried the treasure so that it could not be used. Unlike the Pharisee whose life was walled in by a law, unlike a good deal of conventional piety that would put blinkers on youth—if it could—He set His disciples open-eyed upon the open road, and promised them His company on the Way. The disciples of His choice were men and women ready to stake all on a big venture, taking the days as they came, not worrying overmuch about the future or their future. 'Give us *this day* our daily bread'. 'Be not anxious for the morrow'—what brave reticence!

There is a story in the Gospels which gives us insight into the ethical values of Jesus—the story of the woman in the house of Simon, the Pharisee. Simon is shocked that a good man should not know at once the kind of woman she was, and even more shocked that he did not send her off as soon as he did know. She *was* a sinner —but the qualities which made her liable to certain sins also made her capable of a quality of life which the Pharisee could not achieve. 'Her sins which are many are forgiven, for she loved much.' Similarly, on another occasion: 'Verily, the publicans and harlots go into the Kingdom of Heaven before you,' and again, the parable of the Publican and the Pharisee at their prayers. In these words there is an ethical revaluation and a spiritual truth of great moment. They recognize that a large heart and a generous temper which may land a man in grievous sins have more of the stuff of Christian sainthood than a pigeon-hearted rectitude, and also that the Pharisee, Jewish or Christian, like the elder brother, would be better for a fall or two—more generous and human perhaps—more humble before God and penitent. Falls do not matter so much if a man is walking in the right direction, and is able to pick himself up in humble faith and good courage. 'For she loved much'—this appraisement was not, as the moralist thought, evidence that He was easy-going. It implied a scale of values different, subtly but profoundly different, from that of the Pharisee. And the difference springs from the differing conceptions of the character and activity of God. The robust, venturous ethic of the Gospels is bound up with the ministry of the Holy Spirit and the doctrine of Grace.[1]

In the service of God and man, those who are led by the Spirit of God will not resent to-day's fatigues or be over-anxious about to-morrow's rations. For the Spirit of God in Christ Jesus and in history is an adventurous spirit who seems to take great risks. He has been really very troublesome to theologians, and still more to ecclesiastical administrators, because He always seems to be bursting the bounds they set and the regulations they frame. In His hunger for the love of men He over-leaps even the channels of His own making, just as the Son of Man broke the sacred rule of the Jewish religion to heal and to save. Not only within Christendom but in other religions and 'heathen lands afar', His path may be traced as He lights and leads men by 'unconvenanted mercies' into truth and love. The Spirit of God is the Love seen in the Cross—foolish in the eyes of cultured humanists who have an aversion from suffering and sacrifice and refuse to see divinity in either—offensive to Pharisees who think that God is as proud as they are, and refuse to associate Him with the indignity and recklessness of the Cross.

But the good news of Jesus is precisely this—God stoops to conquer, not in craft to outwit the Devil, as theologians once thought, but in love. To reconcile man to Himself, and man with man, He goes to lengths which seem to cold men absurd and to the self-righteous shocking. It is not enough therefore that the members of the family of God should live safe, blameless, law-abiding lives. The rich young man who had kept the rules of the game from his youth up, would never get his cap

[1] C. J. Barker, *The Way of Life*, p. 229.

because he had no genius for the game. Goodness attracts, virtue becomes dynamic only when they are seasoned with a touch of divine recklessness and fired by sacrificial love. 'As many as are led by the Spirit of God are the sons of God.'

The morality of the Sermon on the Mount very decidedly is not the morality of 'see what a good boy am I'. It is the response of those who have seen the Kingdom and repented, and from repentance pass to great thankfulness and wonder that God, in and through the Sacrifice of Jesus, should give such gifts to men. And so, in the community of those who have been baptized into Christ's death, obligation becomes oblation. The service of men—intelligent, wise, thorough-going, sacrificial—becomes a thank-offering for and to the love of God.

I sometimes think that we are psychologically at fault (though not of course theologically) in confessing our sins so often in church and so generally. We do not really get the burden of them out of our minds and rarely experience that levity of spirit and marvellous sense of release which is so dramatically described in *Pilgrim's Progress* when beside the Cross the burden falls from Christian's back and rolls right away.

This morality of the Sermon on the Mount and the beloved community is the morality of Grace—not I but Christ in me—the morality of twice-born men, who know that from God and to God are all things. The Sermon and the Parables picture the life and ministry in the world of a penitent society, forgiving because it knows at what cost its members have been forgiven. It is indeed an unpractical programme either for an unrepentant Church or a secular world—the new wine will not go into the old skins. So J. A. Findlay writes very truly, 'the Sermon on the Mount, however simple and natural it may be made to look, will always remain hopelessly impracticable if we leave out the motive to which Jesus always makes His first appeal—"he that loveth me keepeth my commandments".' In my early days, idealists and perfectionists ran round arguing that this divine teaching was a body of principles which could be 'applied' to society at large, and might even be carried out by a society which might not hold the faith from which it springs. The idealism that would make it the moral law of a secular society provokes the scepticism of those who take a more realistic view, and encourages them to dismiss Jesus as a vague idealist who sets before men an inspiring ideal which cannot be the working creed of an imperfect world. It would, indeed, be disastrous if both communist and capitalist turned away from the teaching of Jesus in search of rougher tools.

If the teaching is not an ethical code which can be 'applied', neither is it just a vision of a heaven that shall be.[2] No, it is this-worldly in its reference. More by illustration than by report—and with not a little humour—it shows how disciples of the Lord of Life will behave not only towards one another, but also towards all men in a world where fools, knaves, humbugs and evil men abound. It shows how in all the varied relationships and tensions of life, these relations may be kept unbroken and made human if the members of Christ will go to all lengths to keep them human and unbroken. It is a way of life for the saints on earth—a church militant and missionary. The power to live this life and to do this work comes by way of the baptism of repentance and the Cross, dying to live, losing to find—my Grace is sufficient unto thee. The difference between the true Church and a company of moral idealists is that the members of the former community know themselves to be sinners, but sinners walking the road that leads to eternal life, who know their need of God's pardon and love, and thus knowing and seeking, receive by His Grace

[2] Cf. Barker, *ibid.*, p. 227.

power from on high to love as He loves. So the ethical teaching was secondary to the call to know God truly, and to take Him seriously. 'Except you are born again you cannot even see the Kingdom.' 'Have faith in God, and then and not until then will you be able to move mountains.' In the Fourth Gospel, Christian experience has paraphrased those words—'When the Comforter is come, He will convict the world of sin and of righteousness'. 'The Spirit of truth will lead you into all truth.' While St. Paul sums up the ministry of the Christian community in this sentence, 'Always bearing in the body the dying of the Lord Jesus, that the life also of Jesus might be manifest in our body.'

In His dealings with men and women, our Lord does not seem to have said or implied that only after they had reformed themselves and kept straight for some time would they be allowed into His presence, but rather that in His company they would find power to change their way of life and to become new men. He did not expect men to live out, or up to, His way of life apart from Him —independently of God. And so it was. Sinners at whom the moralists looked disapprovingly and who evaded their company were drawn by the forgiveness implicit in the Master's invitation; in His company they saw themselves for what they were, and at the same time gained hope and confidence, without which it is not possible to make a fresh start in life.

The incident of the blind beggar recorded in St. Luke, chapter eighteen, is an example of such love in action, which strikes home every time I read it. The blind man by the wayside; the tramp of feet; the sound of voices— 'Halloa, what's up,' he says to himself. 'How much will they bring in?' He is told, 'Jesus of Nazareth is passing by.' 'Him!' Surprisingly he seizes the opportunity, rightly as well as boldly. He does not ask for alms, but for that which only Jesus could bestow—the pardon of

God. Those in front—maybe the chosen twelve, may be just fellow-travellers—try to shut him up. 'These tiresome beggars, a plague on them! Can't he realize that time presses and the Master has more important things to think about.' Not so Jesus. The progress to Calvary for the redemption of mankind is halted by the cry of a single man in need. 'What do you want me to do for you?' Again the opportunity seized the bold cry of faith—'Lord that I may receive my sight.' He receives his sight.

Christian ministry becomes creative when it is infused with that supreme charity which is not content just to hold out a helping hand, but glimpsing the Christ in every man, woman and child is an identification with the will of the Father and with the joys, sorrows, needs and sins of ordinary folk. As Simone Weil says truly, 'Christ taught us that the supernatural love of our neighbour is the exchange of compassion and gratitude which happens in a flash between two beings, one possessing and the other deprived of human personality.'[3]

The epistles, and the life of the early Church reflected in them, are a wonderful commentary on this teaching in the Gospels. When St. Paul said, 'Be ye imitators of God', and even more boldly, 'Be ye imitators of me as I am of Christ Jesus', he knew, none better, that the new life was not achieved by punctilious copying of a new pattern. It was 'The law of the Spirit of life in Christ Jesus', a new life made possible by Grace to those who had been 'buried with Christ Jesus through baptism unto death that like as Christ rose again from the dead through the glory of the Father, so we also might walk in newness of life'. The near approach of the life of the Church to the teaching of the Gospels was—and always will be—through the fellowship of the Holy Spirit. The individual coming into contact with the society—and not

[3] Simone Weil, *Waiting upon God*, p. 88.

just individuals, whole families and groups—and being received into its friendship, escaped from the past into a new life. Being a penitent society, its corporate ministry was one of forgiveness. In its friendship the new-comer was encouraged to begin again, and better. Unlike the world, it was not a society in which old scores were remembered. It was the whole company of the faithful which was the body of Christ, their common life the embodiment of His, their missionary enterprise the continuing of His ministry. While it might have been difficult and even dangerous for the individual convert to exercise alone the ministry of Jesus to publicans and sinners, seeing that he had only just escaped from their company, it was the ministry of the Church community in which each member had his part and function.[4] The individual finds life as he loses himself in this service to the world; indeed he cannot be in any full sense a Christian except through membership of a society filled with His Spirit and loyal to His ministry of reconciliation and love.

Alas, the churches we know are very dimly such a fellowship. But even as they are, the Church, through its inheritance, through its sacraments, through its prophets, which it often persecutes, and through its saints, does mediate to society a portion of the Spirit that dwelt in her Lord without measure. If, as I believe, the Sermon on the Mount is the morality—the programme, if you like—of the Divine Society, the Church militant here on earth, rather than of groups on a more secular basis, then some of the enthusiasm expended on exhorting secular society to keep its moral standards up might be better spent in trying to get our church communities to practise more completely the Gospel given us to preach. Possibly the only way in which a secular society whose life is too much determined by economic necessity may be saved

[4] See Eph. 4.

from self-destruction, will be by the deeper understanding, commitment and dedication of the membership of the Church to the way of the Cross.

There is a paradox in the life of the Church, nevertheless, as in the earthly ministry of her Lord, which we must not try to smooth away. It has to be a forgiving society receiving into its fellowship men and women who have learned Christ very imperfectly, and therefore it always runs the risk of becoming spiritually impoverished and corrupted by the world. At the same time, by the Grace of God, who uses the weakness of men to glorify Himself, it has to practise a ministry of love, identifying itself with sympathy and imagination and by self-giving with all humanity even as the Lord Jesus did, thereby filling up, as St. Paul boldly said, what was lacking in the afflictions of Christ—a morality of perfection that transcends the morality of my station and my duties, and brings to society the stimulating challenge of a finer quality of life whose pattern is in heaven and whose spring is the very Love of God.

IV

CRUCIAL ISSUES

A. J. Toynbee, in *A Study of History*, writes: 'It may be that in every age of every society some moral issue is always the challenge that is fateful for the society's future.' There are a number of contemporary moral issues—danger spots—in regard to which society may go astray, if there is no Christian vision and insight, and if Christians, corporately and individually, do not act vigorously according to such light as they have—which may not be exclusively theirs. One of these more than the rest may prove to be the issue which is the challenge that Toynbee has in mind or it may be that there is a common element in several issues which is the crucial test. Be that as it may, I propose to set out seven issues of varying magnitude and to discuss them not exhaustively but sufficiently to show what might be a Christian approach to them.

1. *The End and the Means*

The thesis that *the ends justify the means* has had a long life in history. Before and since Machiavelli wrote *Il Principe* it has governed the practice of many statesmen, ecclesiastical and secular. It has betrayed many sincere ideologists into the hands of gangsters. But perhaps it has never been so widely accepted and so pervasive as in our time. The girl who pilfers from her fellow-worker in the factory cloak-room; the worker who scrounges a piece of wood or steel from the works for his own use; the business man who fails to honour a promise if it is no longer to his advantage; the totalitarian state, which rounds up in concentration camps those it suspects, makes its prisoners slaves, and subjects its opponents to torture; a priest who argues that, as a priesthood is necessary and the Church must be kept going, it is legitimate to raise money by betting and gambling; a Church which in defence and in aggression employs the weapons of the world and has in fact taught the world the mechanics of totalitarianism; all these, at their different levels, consciously or unconsciously, are exemplary of the thesis that the ends justify the means. And of them all the last is the worst offender—*corruptio optima pessima*—for the Lord Jesus endured the Cross rather than assent to this plausible and deadly untruth.

Looking more closely at the examples I have taken, one finds that the girl or the man who pilfers is assuming that she or he is in fact 'number one'—and therefore her or his desires are the first and overriding consideration in every situation. 'What makes me content or what suits my convenience, is what determines my conduct, and the test that I apply is subjective, emotional, immediate.' The totalitarian state—or rather those who control it—argue that the continued and successful existence of the state is the first priority—in the long run, that is the greatest benefit which it confers on its citizens—therefore it must be quite ruthless and undeviating in the exercise of power, especially over the social units that compose it.[1] The priest argues that the Church of God, its triumphs and glories, are the end of life, and the means of salvation, therefore the ethical perfection of the end exonerates any short-comings in the means employed to strengthen the Church's position and influence in the world. An act which, considered in

[1] Lenin is reported to have said, 'There are no morals in politics; there is only expediency.'

isolation from the ultimate end it serves, might be considered evil, is transformed into good, or at least into a justifiable instrument for the good, by the end which it is serving.

So runs the thesis. Its strength lies in its plausibility—the better the end the more plausible it becomes. If the story of the Temptation be read as autobiography then it is clear that our Lord Himself felt its strength as well as its insidious danger. He resisted it and the price of His resistance was crucifixion. The Cross stands as an uncompromising challenge to those who would do evil that good may come. It is for the soldiers of the Cross to attack this plausible lie wherever it raises its head.[2]

The ends which a man or community serve will, broadly, determine the means that he employs to further them. Occasionally the means may rise superior to the end as, for example, when a man makes heroic sacrifices for a cause which is unworthy and false, though it may not be so in his eyes. The Christian should be passionately concerned that men should serve right ends, and he should be deeply assured by the Word of God that the right end is not individual egoism, or democracy or tyranny or the State or the Church as an organization, but the Kingdom of God. Man's chief end is to glorify God and enjoy Him for ever—and all the means that he uses should be congruous with that end. This for two reasons. Life should be a unity of means and ends, and not disconnected fragments. The way a man acts and reacts to the day-to-day demands of life should be a

[2] Mr. Barker in *The Way of Life*, makes the same point in these words: 'It is notable that our Lord invariably refused to employ means that were ethically incompatible with the end sought. His temptation in the wilderness was concerned with using means that were alien to the end He had in view. At the very end He refused to attempt to inaugurate a Kingdom not of this world with the weapons of this world. His followers have not been so consistent,' (p. 216).

pointer towards the ends he serves—a symbol, a sacrament of the Kingdom that shall be. It was impossible for the true son of God to cast out devils by the power of Beelzebub. It was equally impossible for the Son of God to achieve the purpose of His incarnate life by stooping to conquer by means which the world and the devil might put into His hands. In the second place, the methods which are used to achieve the victory of love, should themselves illustrate and embody love, so that they bear their own witness to the true end of life, and convince others both of its value and also of the complete integrity of the man who serves it.

The Christian and the Churchman, therefore, have to be clear in regard to the end of life. Jesus is the Way, and therefore His followers must be finely sensitive in their self-criticism, and strive to make all their ways in harmony with the Way of Him who is truth and life. They have to enlighten the eyes of men to see the true end of life, and help them to seek it honestly without hypocrisy and dissembling and not allow them to be allured by what appears the plausible short-cut of adopting a dubious means because it may promise quick returns. To all such siren voices the voice of Christ says, 'Get thee behind me, Satan, for thou savourest not the things of God but of men'. The greatest failures of the Church and its priesthood have been due to their readiness to be more worldly-wise; but God's battles are never won by such means.

In life, however, there are secondary and temporary ends to be served as well as the ultimate end, which is the Kingdom of God. As citizen, a man has to serve the welfare of the state. If he should be a responsible statesman he has to see that the government is carried on and order preserved. If he is an industrial manager he has to see that the business is efficient and successful. A parent has to maintain his family. In some of these roles a Christian will have to co-operate with men who may not share his belief about the true end of life and the true way to live. What then shall the righteous do if they cannot contract out of the life of the world? A state arms itself and perhaps goes to war in order to defend itself against an aggressor. A Christian who is not a perfectionist, before he acquiesces and supports such a choice of evils, will try to assure himself that that is the real reason and not just a pretence to cover its own aggression. He also ought to recognize that force can only withstand force and cannot achieve positive good. He also ought to be resistant to the poisons of propaganda and the fevers of hatred. Whether in domestic life in support of his family, or in the life of the community, once a man allows that a good end can be achieved by objectionable means—a just cause by doing unjustly by a human being—he stands on as slippery a slope as the Gadarene swine ran down. What happened in Germany under Hitler illustrates most tragically the way in which once evil means are allowed they surely deflect and corrupt the ends until both these and the means become depraved and militantly evil. The history of Communism since the death of Lenin may one day be found to provide the same example and lesson.

2. *Responsibility and Freedom*

'The price of any freedom,' Michael Roberts wrote in *The Recovery of the West,* 'is the acceptance of responsibility.' It is precisely at this point that Industrial Society is showing signs of breaking down—and in more ways than one. There is the moral irresponsibility exemplified in the number of easily broken marriages, the extent of pilfering and juvenile delinquency, about which our moralists are vocal. But these are epi-phenomena of mass-society in the aftermath of war. More fundamental is the fact to which insufficient attention has been paid that the industrial revolution brought into existence an industrial society in which, for five or six generations now, the majority of the population has been denied responsibility and has thereby been made irresponsible. They do not want responsibility. They want security, shorter hours, better wages; they are decent chaps, good workmen, most of them; but they are not interested in the real issues of industrial organization and politics, and many couldn't care less. They leave to a small minority the responsibility of exercising its mind on these; in so far as they exercise their minds on anything, it is on such matters as football pools. Some time ago, I spent an evening with a dozen shop stewards in the steel industry and they were lamenting how little real interest they could get out of the men in larger issues. T.U. secretaries will regretfully admit that men will pay their weekly contribution and walk away from the branch's meeting as soon as they have done it, taking not the slightest interest in the meeting as such. There is nothing new in this. It is an inevitable consequence of the first 150 years of industrial development when for several generations the wage-earner was just 'a hand', liable to be paid off at short notice, driven by economic circumstances to live from hand to mouth and to think accordingly. It will take more than a few years to change the psychological consequences and a mental attitude which has become endemic. None the less, the altered status of the manual worker makes this inability or unwillingness of the many to accept responsibility a serious matter.

It is, unfortunately, a state of mind not confined to him, but runs through society and is found in men and women at all economic levels because other causes are operating to make people reluctant to accept responsibility. One is the scale—the sheer size of the industrial machine. A boy or girl leaving school, where they have been the centre of the picture, and going into industry feels one of a crowd lost in a crowd, and easily falls into the mental attitude of 'I couldn't care less'. The machine is so vast, their part in it so small, that their concern becomes limited to the wage-packet.

In the wider sphere of politics, the same influences operate. Two world wars and all that follows make the ordinary man feel helpless, a creature of necessity. Beyond politics, and in measure determining politics, are theories of human life which set human values at a discount and reckon the individual of small account. Such influences are prejudicial to a free democracy: they make it possible for small determined minorities to get hold of the controls: they make the way of dictators easy. For freedom can only be had and held at the price of 'the voluntary acceptance of responsibility'.

It would not be difficult to arrive at a similar conclusion from a consideration of the cultural life of an industrial society in which the demand for adult education is small; the popular Press makes no appeal to the reasoning powers of its readers, and popular amusements require little active response from those they amuse. In such a *milieu* it is not surprising that a religious faith which speaks in terms of purpose and its consequent ethic which requires the acceptance of responsibility have not the appeal of 'good news'.

What then shall the righteous do? First note in passing some things which are being done. There are industrial undertakings where attempts are being made, not without success, to stimulate the interest of the young worker in the total life and product, so that although only engaged in one shop, perhaps even in a repetitive process, he or she may see the whole of which it is a part. Works Councils, when they are well used, also spread responsibility. Moreover, at a higher level both the T.U.C. and Industrial Management are becoming more alive to the problem. Again, the increase of 'higher education', if it embodies the higher values in culture and life, may in time increase the number of those who will accept responsibility when given it. After all, it is the giving of responsibility which is the best way of making a person realize that much is required of him. But the solution, I submit, will not be found in education or in industrial reorganization unless it is also sought on the spiritual level at the same time.

The sense of helplessness and drift which follows upon the enthronement of Chance and Necessity as the sovereign powers in life—which is our contemporary *malaise*—is in sharp contrast to the Christian doctrines of the purpose of God and the reality of sin. 'While the sense of drift,' Toynbee writes, 'has the effect of an opiate in instilling acquiescence in an evil which is assumed to reside in external circumstances beyond the victim's control, the sense of sin has the effect of a stimulus because it tells the sinner that the evil is within him and is therefore subject to his will—if only he wills to carry out God's purpose and to render himself accessible to God's grace. There is here the whole difference between the Slough of Despond in which Christian for a time wallowed and the original impetus which started him running towards "yonder wicket gate".' So far Toynbee, and it is well said. The sense of sin is the obverse of a sense of purpose. When there comes to a man or woman the conviction that life has a purpose in which he and she have a share, then they may do the day's work with constancy, and when they fail to do it may have a troubled conscience. 'My Father works and I work,' said Jesus. Although the ordinary man may hardly think of his job like that, nevertheless the best work is done by men who believe that they are contributing to a worth-while purpose, and that not just their own, and are prepared in some measure to go short and to work over-time in order to serve true ends.

If our civilization is to survive it must be reinforced by a new Christian culture, itself the flowering of a finer quality of life. Industry and democracy demand for their success a sense of responsibility widely shared, and a will to work for the common good. It will be imparted to the generality of men and women, so largely imitative in their habits, by a creative minority, who accept a compulsion beyond their own wills and desires in the choices they make in life. The day's work as 'community service' is not enough: it may only be fine words. A work and a life in which a man spends himself because he recognizes his dependence on God and honestly believes that what he is doing is the way of using his talents and opportunities most agreeable with the divine purpose —that is a creative thought and action. It is raised to the highest level when the choice is sacrificial, and the Cross of Jesus Christ is its light and inspiration.

It is in vocation that all that is true in individualism comes into its own, and vocation and the acceptance of responsibility tie into one another. I believe that it will be the growth once again of a sense of vocation in the community coeval with the growth of the welfare state which will keep the latter true to its name, and will increase the sense of responsibility among the many, and correct abuses of power on the part of the few. But at bottom, vocation is a response to God, a God who acts in life, a God who declared Himself in the ministry and cross of Jesus. Therefore, before all else, men have to be helped to identify Him at work in His world, and to become aware of His activity in their own experience and in history; and in Jesus Christ to see the pattern of life and to receive from Him the power to reproduce it.

It is the function of the Church, not just the one per cent who are clergy, but also the ninety-nine per cent who are laity, to be the creative minority in society, its own worship and life renewed by the Spirit of God. The Bible from first to last exposes the relationship between God and Church as a covenanted relationship. That is why both Testaments expound man's life so strongly in terms of responsibility and insist that to whom much is given, from him much is required. The more elevated the conception of the character of the God who enters into covenant with man, the more will man's response be lifted from the level of duty to that of love—but the fact of covenant remains. It runs like a thread through the ethical teaching of the Gospel; it is a constant in the religion of St. Paul. 'For though I be free from all men, yet have I made myself servant unto all that I might gain the more'—'freely ye have received, freely give'—dedicated lives. A body of Christians which is not greatly occupied in its own defences, so intent is it upon its ministry to society, will approve its own faith, because by God's grace it will create the quality of life that matches men and women to their responsibilities. But the warning stands, enforced by the history of civilizations: 'For I say unto you that unto everyone who hath shall be given: and from him that hath not, even that he hath shall be taken from him.'

3. *The Use and Abuse of Power*

> 'The love of power amounts to a desire to establish order among men and things around oneself, either on a large scale or small scale, and this desire for order is a result of a sense of beauty.'[3]

This penetrating judgment by Simone Weil not only explains why many tyrants in the past have, like the

[3] Simone Weil, *Waiting on God*, p. 105.

Medicis, been men of culture and lovers of beauty, it also marks the place from which many dictators in state, industry, school and family have started. The distaste of men or women with ability and force of personality for living and working in a mess; their vision of society as a hierarchy of order with a master-mind in ultimate control; and their consequent desire to organize and direct, these are not necessarily evil, and may be beneficent. Power, nevertheless, subtly but surely can run away with such men and women if it entwines itself with their egoism and selfishness and is not severely controlled by patience and humility, self-discipline and love. Few men are so well-endowed with these qualities as to be able to enjoy the exercise of much power over their fellows without coming to enjoy it too much. When that process sets in moral decline and corruption follow.

What is true of individuals is even more true of groups. The impersonal exercise of power by a group of men will become more callous and cruel than the individual member of such a group might be if he were on his own. The member of such a group can excuse to himself the ruthlessness of their corporate decisions by his loyalty to the group; similarly a subordinate member of a dictatorship will justify evil-doing by his loyalty to the dictator. Industrial history and modern politics—to look no further afield—will supply many examples of this corruption.

Modern techniques have placed immense powers beyond the dreams of old-time tyrants within the grasp of men to-day. A minority once it has captured the key positions in a state can rarely be unseated by rebellion from within the state. Therefore the right use of power has become a major issue of our time. Radio, press, film, television, rapid transport, education, social services, can one and all be used to condition and to control the minds of men and to destroy freedom. The Kremlin is doing this with a thoroughness that makes the tyrannies of the past appear like nursery games, and the dictatorships of Hitler and Mussolini adolescent experiments. By liquidating opponents or by large scale mass slavery, by ruthless control of information and of freedom of thought, by the devices of deification (of the dictator), by a most complete autocracy, the Kremlin is trying to make all Russia and its satellites think, march, worship one way. It is a terrifying experiment, because even if that particular dictatorship were to fail, it shows the menacing power which a godless scientism might exercise in the world.

'To my mind,' writes Karl Stern in *The Pillar of Fire*, 'there is only one form of society which is worse than the Marxist or the Fascist one, that is precisely—a scientific one. Needless to say that there is nothing wrong with economics or political science or psycho-analysis or social science or any other similar subject. The great Russian thinkers of the nineteenth century who were so distrustful and hostile towards science mixed science (which is precious) up with scientism (which is destructive). It is this scientism as a norm of human life, without God as a centre, which leads to a form of nihilism unequalled in history. . . . There are indications that secularism and pragmatism, which have by comparison led a rather amateurish existence outside Russia, may be shaped into some scientific-technocratic norm for human beings. This, not material destruction, would mean the end of mankind.'[4]

Modern techniques, and especially propaganda which can sell the lie with appalling success, should make

[4] *Ibid.*, pp. 292-3. The whole passage should be read—indeed the whole of this remarkable story of a life.

Christians sensitively critical of power pressures in every sphere of life.

A Protestant, and I use the word in the strict sense of one who protests, not against the sacramental truth of catholicism, but against the dictatorship of the Vatican, is bound to see with deepening anxiety the way in which the Vatican is being driven by the logic of its assumptions to use modern techniques, not only to control more rigorously the minds of Roman Catholics and to direct the policies of that Church in every country in the world, but also to pursue *a strategy of penetration in the political life of every country*, which becomes in some countries a virtual veto upon all criticism in print or on the air. The Papacy is the oldest totalitarian power in the world. It 'differs from that of the state because it has a spiritual content and a spiritual purpose completely lacking in the latter'.[5] This makes it both stronger and weaker. Stronger, because of its claim to be able to formulate and prescribe all truth necessary for man's salvation—'We who hold upon this earth the place of God Almighty' (Leo XIII in his letter on *The Reunion of Christendom*)—and also because in the pageantry of Rome the Pope is the centre of the picture and is glorified to a degree far excelling the exaltation of any secular monarch. Weaker because the Papacy cannot exercise physical force except indirectly through a subservient state. In the Middle Ages, in spite of primitive methods of transport and slow communications, the Papacy was for a long time able to control men's thought and did not hesitate to employ—indirectly—cruelty and torture to stamp out heresy. If in the sixteenth century the Papacy had had the technical resources at its disposal which it has to-day, the Inquisition might have been able to prevent the Protestant Reformation. It is because the battle

[5] Professor Le Piana of Harvard University, quoted by Paul Blanshard, cf. *infra*.

which the Roman Church is fighting against Communism is politically a conflict between two totalitarian powers—Kremlin and Papacy—employing up to a point the same sort of power pressures and making the same sort of claim to control the thoughts and exact the obedience of men—that Protestant Christians who believe that democracy is a political expression of Christian values cannot identify themselves with Rome in its conduct of this contest.[6]

The report of the Economic section of the Conference on Church, Community and State at Oxford in 1937,[7] analysed the irresponsible use of power in the economic sphere, which was the great evil of *laissez-faire* capitalism. More recent and effective controls have not made that discussion academic. It is the power that wealth makes possible rather than the luxuries and pleasures that money can buy which makes some men covetous. To-day in industry and in the state it is possible to exercise great power without having or caring much about great riches. The surgeons of the Kremlin may not be rich, but they are immensely powerful—and such power is a glittering prize above all wealth.

Idealists have paid insufficient attention to the power motive. Sir George Schuster, in *Christianity and Human Relations in Industry*, writes, 'I believe that "the power motive" or the "publicity motive" may be even more dangerous than the "profit motive"—certainly more than the profit motive as now limited and controlled.'[8] Power exercised by individuals and groups over other

[6] The parallels (and the differences) between the dictatorships of the Kremlin and the Papacy are fully explored in Professor Paul Blanshard's last book, *Communism, Democracy and Catholic Power*, Beacon Press, Boston, U.S.A., 1951.

[7] *The Churches Survey their Task*, Allen and Unwin. The Economic Report is published separately as a pamphlet.

[8] *Christianity and Human Relations in Industry*, The Beckley Lectures for 1951, Epworth Press, p. 102.

individuals and groups tends to corrupt the exploited as well as the exploiters. What Bertrand Russell[9] calls 'the unconscious arrogancy of power' is, indeed, uglier in its effect upon the exploited. The man of power often has a way with him that is attractive; not so the servility of the exploited or the truculence of those who fear that exploitation may make them servile.

Social administration in recent times has been tending to transfer power from voluntary groups to statutory authorities, and from local authorities to the central authority in a country. Whitehall to-day has more day to day control over the lives of Englishmen than Henry VIII had—though the fact is disguised by better manners and made acceptable by good service. The tendency is made inevitable both by the complexity of modern society and by its easy communications, but it has to be watched critically. In state as in church the distribution of power is the safeguard against totalitarianism and is essential to democracy.

Unless the exercise of power is determined and disciplined by a true understanding of the nature and destiny of man, which Christianity gives, it will do more evil than good. The God of Christ's revelation declares His power 'most chiefly in showing mercy and pity' (Collect for the eleventh Sunday after Trinity). Christian faith finds that exercise of power worshipful. Christian belief, supported by experience, is sure that power so used, and only if it is so used, makes for true community and happiness among men. This faith and belief have been mediated through Jesus Christ who set before men a new conception of kingship and power, and also of the dignity of meekness. In refusing the temptation to coerce the minds and wills of men and in preferring the persuasion of truth, goodness and love He chose for Himself the Cross. And this King who reigns from the Cross

[9] Bertrand Russell. *Power: A Social Analysis.*

has kept His authority down the centuries as secular and ecclesiastical potentates who reign from thrones have failed to do.

The judgment that the meek are blessed and shall inherit the earth is an ultimate judgment which the natural history of men and beasts only upholds occasionally. 'The ultimate judgments of religion upon the strong and the weak, the proud and the humble,' Niebuhr has written, 'are momentarily defied with impunity, but ultimately validated in history.'[10] Pride and naked power lead to injustice; injustice when it reaches a degree of excess, raises up forces that overthrow the exploiter. That dialectic process seems to run through history. In our time the last term in the process has become more difficult and much more costly in human suffering. Nevertheless, the destruction that the unbridled will-to-power and injustice bring upon themselves in time is, perhaps, the most providential element in history. Nietzsche, who scorned Christianity as the vengeance of the slaves upon their masters, glorified the will-to-power as 'the basic vitality of existence'. Nietzsche was the prophet of the dictators: the last word remains with the Son of Man who was among men as one that serveth.

What then should be the Christian approach to the use of power?

First, Christians should recognize the fact of power, and also realize that in modern society there is more of it than there used to be. Consequently, the right use of power will do more good, and the wrong use will do more evil than once upon a time. The use of power has therefore to be approached, treated and regulated objectively, rationally, scientifically, as far as possible in the economic

[10] Cf. Niebuhr, *The Nature and Destiny of Man*, and especially the sections on the Sin of Pride, Collective Egoism, and, in the second volume, on history.

and political sphere as in the physical. The longer the fact of power and its use can be kept from intruding into the moral sphere the better. The tension, for example, within industry between the vesting of executive power in one man or a small board for the sake of efficiency and order, and the spreading of responsibility among the many to safeguard freedom and equity is just a fact of life. It need not become a moral issue if it were treated with scientific objectivity. It becomes a moral issue when the love of power on the one side, or the fear of exploitation, or may be a refusal to accept responsibility on the other, throws things off balance. Idealists and social reformers are apt not to see power until it is abused, and then we discuss its use too exclusively in ethical terms. The use of power becomes a moral issue when its exercise is ill-regulated, when, for example, in a country it becomes over-centralized, and in consequence the love of power can be over-indulged.

Secondly, therefore, a Christian will exercise a heroic watchfulness over himself and his mental processes, more especially if he is in a position to mould and dominate other minds and direct other lives—pupils, employees, members of his family, citizens. 'The supernatural virtue of justice,' to quote Simone Weil again, 'consists of behaving exactly as though there were equality when one is the stronger in an unequal relationship. . . . He who treats as equal those who are far below him in strength really makes them a gift of the quality of human beings, of which fate had deprived them.'[11]

Thirdly, he will maintain a critical judgment of modern techniques and tendencies, especially in the sphere of thought control and propaganda. He will wisely and boldly expose abuses of power, and in co-operation with others, will resist the exploiters. Who

[11] *Ibid.*, p. 86.

can deny that the Church has often been not only too docile towards them, but one of them?

Fourthly, a Christian will refuse to accept an order of society where social injustice and irresponsible use of power are approved or too easily tolerated. Positively, it will work for a social order where each individual is 'treated in such a way that he has the possibility of choosing to love God, and social life is organized so that each aspect of it becomes a sacrament—and this because he knows that in God's world "souls must not be mutilated unnecessarily by enslavement and poverty".'[12] While too much cannot be expected of human nature or even of minds enlightened by sciences until they are being taught by Jesus Christ, the Christian ought to strive to influence the prevailing currents in society so that they help rather than hinder Christian living.

And fifthly, churchmen will ever be mindful that the Church should exemplify the values that it proclaims to be true. Its authorities should rule in love; its priests should be clothed not in pride but in righteousness; its own economy just and wise, without abuse of power and money—a pattern to the world because its members know their citizenship to be in heaven. And for that reason, knowing that they are sinful and fallible men living in an imperfect world, they will not claim for any human tribunal an infallibility that belongs only to the Triune God or identify the Church on earth with the Kingdom of God.

4. *The Attraction of Money*

Since the beginning of history riches have been a corrupting as well as a cultural influence in life. Our Lord

[12] These words are from a review of Simone Weil's *Attente de Dieu* in the October issue of *The Twentieth Century*.

spoke much about it; His disciples have often turned a deaf ear to that part of His teaching. The love of riches and the power they give a man over his fellow-men, however, are not precisely what I have in mind. A new factor in modern life has been introduced by the availability to the many of facilities and resources which in times past were only available for the few. As a result of scientific discoveries and new industrial techniques, there is available a range of amusements, interests, activities and material possessions such as society has never known before. Travel, sport, cultural activities, food and drink, household goods, amusements, entertainment—all these are available *provided you have the cash.* Shouting at men and women from the hoardings, from the press, and in some countries on the radio, are voices telling them how much there is for their money to buy. And unless a man has money for buying, life can become insipid and thin, and even a lonely business. Therefore everybody wants money, and lots of it—that is part of the appeal of football pools and the like. They want it more acutely than their forbears did because it can make life nowadays so rich and interesting. The churches want it as much as the rest—many of them are not doing as well as they might because they are so short of it.

This desire for an ever-rising standard of life is not just cupidity. But what are you going to do about it? How does it stand in relation to our Lord's warning 'Be not anxious for meat, drink and raiment', and to His assurance 'Seek first the Kingdom of God and all these things shall be added to you?' At what point should desire be curbed, and why? Most of our sermons about money are out of date, for they do not come to grips with the way in which Mammon has turned himself into a fairy godmother and a universal aunt, or with the new tension and unrest in social life which are in consequence arising.

There is also emerging a temporary problem for which

British society is not well prepared. Full employment and good wages will not yield the fruits expected of them if there is a scarcity of goods for ordinary consumers and if high productive and distributive costs put them beyond the reach of most people. This predicament may arrive in Britain if a large part of the income of the state and the work of its people for several years have to be devoted to armaments; it might also happen through economic maladjustments in the world which would hit a country so dependent on overseas trade. We do not know what would be the psychological effects of such a predicament on the people or what steps might be taken to mitigate its effects. The situation would be different from that created by mass unemployment. The unemployment crisis caught the Church without a common mind or a policy; let us try to look ahead and not be caught so unprepared and unhelpful by the next crisis that may come.

A visitor to North America from Europe is struck not so much by the plentiful supply of goods which in his own country are scarce—that he expected—but by the taking for granted, and accepting as necessary, of amenities and of technical and material standards, which are far from common to the rest of mankind. It has been reckoned that if the average consumption of petrol in America were the average for the whole world, the world's supply would be exhausted in two years. There are two issues here. The first is the tension in human and and national relationships caused by a different standard of wealth, comfort, and the necessaries of life within the world's economy, and the difference in salary scales which ensues. On account of this the United States continually draws off the population of Canada into itself. On account of this its army is not as popular as one would expect in countries where its members are stationed, except among its immediate clients. Even if a most generous estimate is made of the actual and potential value of 'the Estate of Man', it cannot be fairly shared without levelling down as well as levelling up. Moreover some of the marketable wealth of America is due not merely to efficient production but also to using up of capital resources.[13]

The other issue is the tendency of all this to turn Christians into hedonists, and to evacuate Christianity of its ascetic other-worldly element. The worship of the dollar is not necessarily restricted to those who live in the sterling area. Can the Christian Church keep a cutting edge on its faith and life if its members are too comfortably cushioned? What is the relation between the way of the Cross and the way of life which sets a high value on material things, and therefore on money? It is too soon to make dogmatic judgments, but there is an issue here which must not be evaded by the assumption that modern techniques have at last made it possible for modern man to worship God *and* mammon with a good conscience. Perhaps only a Franciscan movement can restore us to a clear perception and practice of the Christian priorities in life.

I cannot leave this subject without reference to the ordained ministry and the circumstances in which men with small fixed incomes are placed. Let me refer again to Sir Wyndham Deedes. When that distinguished soldier and diplomat returned to this country from the Near East, he gave up his family home in Kent and lived in Bethnal Green, making with his gallant mother a home there for social workers and the like in the dreary

[13] Cf. *The Estate of Man*, by the late Michael Roberts (Faber & Faber), pp. 51-2 and elsewhere. 'We have removed the forests as we would coal from a mine with little thought of a new crop.' Paper has become a very expensive part of book production, and in Europe newsprint is limited; but last September I observed that the Sunday edition of the *New York Times* contained 168 pages, together with two smaller-paged supplements of 72 pages in all.

East End of London. He himself lived with the utmost frugality, getting his books from the Public Library, and making use, as he said one ought to do in a society like ours, of such public services as there are without requiring special treatment. It was a notable example and act of witness. It serves to remind us that we have to distinguish between clerical impoverishment, which cripples our ministry, and clerical poverty, which has always characterized the Christian ministry when it has been most persuasive, and which has been a strong element in its power of persuasion. Referring to the ejection of Puritan ministers in 1662, F. D. Maurice wrote, 'The sufferings of these men awakened in the trading class a belief in qualities which they would not otherwise have recognized, a respect for the want of gold which it was the temptation to idolize.'[14] This is the more likely in an industrial society which sets even greater store on money and the range of things which money can provide to-day. There is required of priests, and especially of the women who marry them, patience, sacrifice and unworldliness; and also more intelligence than many of us apply in order that home life may not become monochrome and narrow in range of interests. There are still hobbies which are not costly, and pleasures which money cannot buy, and even close to our cities nature can be found unrationed and free, as those who seek will find.

5. *Work*

Many of the most intractable of present-day problems centre upon work and the incentives to work. The Biblical theologians say that work is 'God's law for man'. Less ponderously one might say that work is a

[14] Maurice, *Representation and Education of the People*, p. 128, quoted by H. G. Wood, *Frederick Denison Maurice*, p. 165.

fact of life; if men and beasts do not work, they starve. Even the grasshopper and the cricket, who were for Æsop idlers *par excellence*, occasionally stop their cricketing to collect a little food for their queer little bodies. Moreover, work, ranging from the creative work of the artist to that of the naked savage tapping coconuts, is an activity which brings men into touch with God who made him. 'My Father worketh and I work,' said the Son of Man, and all the sons of men in their degree should rejoice that they can say and do likewise.

The natural indolence of the oriental made him incline to the view that the law of work was the punishment for man's disobedience, but in truth it is a condition of his sonship and follows from the fact that he was made in the Divine image. Nor does it take us far beyond platitude, or help us to solve contemporary problems, to be told by Canon Richardson, in a recent article on the biblical doctrine of work, that 'the consequence of man's disobedience to God's law is that work, which ought to have been a congenial and salutary human activity, has become a discipline and a task to be endured under the sanctions of force or fear or under the stimuli of profit or reward.[15] If he means that all the difficulties and problems of industrial society are due to the imperfections of human nature, and would be solved if all mankind were in a state of grace, that seems to me just theological boloney. The complex, world-wide, economic and political structure of modern society is quite beyond the horizon of the biblical writers. The Bible is not a text-book for the solution of such problems —though it may provide apposite texts—only the Holy Spirit can lead men to their solving.

The differences between the biblical and the classical attitudes to work, both of which have contributed to Christian tradition, cause a good deal of confusion in our

[15] *The Frontier*, March 1951, p. 114.

thinking. The Bible has a wholesome respect for all honest toil, be it of the hand or of the head. It is seemly that the psalmist should have been a shepherd, the prophet a herdsman and gardener, the Son of God a carpenter. Work is a necessity and every man's work is his service to his neighbour, and his share of a common obligation binding together family and society. The service is not less pleasant if the task is rough and disagreeable. Aristotle's test of a good life, on the other hand, was 'activity according to the standard of excellence'. If that standard were estimated without reference to social justice and a man's duty to his neighbour, it would merely be a functional excellence like art for art's sake. None the less, Greek thought supplies something lacking in biblical thought, and therefore the thorough-going effort of some contemporary theologians to unscramble the biblical and classical strains in our Christian tradition and try to eliminate the latter is regrettable.

The Bible concentrates on the drama of redemption and on the doings of men on two hundred or so square miles of the earth's surface. In so far as the writers give thought to the beauty of the world and the totality of creation it is as a stage-setting for this drama. Beauty for them was not one of the absolutes, nor were they finely sensitive to what one believes is the Creator's joy in *all* created things and in the functional excellence of His creative activity. Even the Apostolic compilers of the Gospel were minded to record only two sayings of our Lord which express this divine love for the beauty of the world.

Man falls short, however, of the perfection of God when his thought and worship limit that perfection to God's redemptive action in history or would confine His love to the baptized members of the new Israel. The universality of God's love is as mysterious and worshipful as its particularity. It does not make sense of the universe if one, so to say, regards it merely as the stuff out of which the armaments of the Church militant are fashioned. The beauty of the world has an absolute excellence of its kind. 'With the exception of God,' Simone Weil writes, 'nothing short of the universe as a whole can with complete accuracy be called beautiful.' Workmanship has an intrinsic value, quite independent of social utility or moral purpose, for it is man's counterpart of the creative activity of God in whose image he is made. The scientist, the technician, the tradesman, like the musician, are glorifying their Creator, whether they are aware of it or not, in their absorption in what they are doing. There is a functional excellence which is a true end in itself. Nevertheless it is not the whole truth. In an imperfect society there must be a confusion of ends unless they can be held consciously in tension. The Christian has to remind the craftsman and the technician as well as the *élite* of industry that they must also ask themselves: For whom am I producing; is the product for my neighbour's and for society's good? A perfectly beautiful atomic bomb is an insufficient answer. They have also to ask of human relationships in a factory (as Mr. W. G. Symons has pointed out): Are we getting together in the best possible way to see this job through?

While giving full heed to these criteria, let Christians not forget that, ideally, work should be worship—an act which can be offered without blasphemy to God who is Creator of the Universe and Source of Wisdom and Science as well as Redeemer. They, of all men, should not acquiesce lightly in utilitarian or in solely ethical standards for human labour.

The problems in regard to work which industrial society is not yet in the way of solving are, in the main, three.

(*a*) In this rapidly-growing technical civilization men

are being compelled to adapt their rhythm to that of the machine. This is a new phenomenon in history if we except the forced labour of slave-gangs. Man's natural rhythm is represented by an undulating line; it is a varying *tempo*—spells of energy alternating with rest. The machine's rhythm is represented by a straight line; it is a uniform *tempo* and regular beat—the conveyor belt. The industrial worker to-day, enslaved to the machine, is doing violence to his nature. It is, therefore, not surprising that he does not find in his work a reminder of his Creator and that, on the contrary, it inclines him, when he reflects, to ruthless and materialistic ideologies. I am disposed to think that an element in the small, sporadic strikes of recent times, and in absenteeism, is a subconscious protest of human beings against the inhumanity of the machine and against their enslavement to it. The solution of this problem in which many of our troubles and infidelities have their roots is hard to see. Increase of leisure may alleviate but it will not solve. For, however reduced hours of work may become, that which provides man with his livelihood will always be the most determinative influence upon his personality and upon his outlook on life. It was for this reason, I surmise, that Maurice argued that leisure is possibly less favourable to learning than work.[16]

(*b*) While it is good that as much brute labour should be transferred to the machine as possible, it is not so good for civilized living that mass-production should take the place of good tradesmanship, and that the consumers' range of choice should be restricted to a small range of utilities. Specialization within the industrial process, however, has for better or worse come to stay. One function of management is to make repetitive work as interesting as possible and to help everyone to take an intelligent interest in and feel some responsibility for the

[16] H. G. Wood, *ibid.*, p. 146.

total product. That is not easy to do when the emphasis in society is so much on profits and the wage-packet and not enough on the satisfaction of work well done and of a service rendered to society. May one whose relation to industry is only that of a consumer be allowed to ask if those in industry are sufficiently conscious of those for whom they are producing? The knowledge that they are producing things necessary to a wholesome and full life might help to reconcile them to the inevitable dullness of much daily work—the housewife's and the clerk's as well as the work of the man and woman in the factory. Here the Christian might set a pattern and the ministry of the Church an example. Unfortunately the Church has been incurably middle-class in its deliverances upon work. Before we can talk to the manual workers at all we must get within talking distance and have more of them within the Christian community.

Although it does not fall precisely within a discussion of Christian morals, I must take leave to say that the separation of the mass of the manual workers and their representatives from the Church in this country is a great evil, and as menacing to the well-being of society as any of the moral evils we have had in mind. And it has largely been the fault of the Churches, for it has not only been our Christianity that has kept them away, but our lack of it. Too few churchmen are vividly aware of this gulf, or care deeply about it. Consequently to the working man in Sheffield or Glasgow, unless he happens to be an Irish Roman Catholic, the church community is another social group—not of his sort. That being the situation, it is no good for churchmen complacently to sit tight until he breaks his way in. He has no desire to break his way in. He has to be met where he is, among his pals, on the shop-floor and in the club. Moreover it will not do just to draw the odd individual out of his group into our church-group; the Church will have, so to say, to baptize, as in its early days and as on the mission field, whole groups into Christian fellowship. And before we are able to do that we shall have to get rid of the remains of snobbery and the lack of imagination which prevent our churches being the classless societies which the family of God should be.

(*c*) Finding incentives to work and overcoming men's distaste for many kinds of work in a day of social security and full employment, when there is an exceptional demand for increased production, is an actual and urgent issue. If our industrial production is to become sufficiently stream-lined to keep pace with that of some other countries then there must be closer, more intelligent and unsuspicious co-operation between all groups in industry, leading to a better quality and quantity of output. That means forgetting some bad memories and old prejudices and acquiring a new outlook. Some bad habits have been created by Trade Union restrictions which were a direct consequence of insecurity and bad conditions of employment. It will take a generation or more to work that particular poison out of the system of industrial society. Another hindrance to economical production has been the regulations resulting from the competition for membership between Trade Unions, e.g. if a small emergency repair involving a lead pipe, a copper pipe, and a bit of joinery has to be done in Britain, a plumber, a fitter, and a joiner have to be assembled on the job. Some people seem to enjoy work for work's sake more than others—the Germans, for example, more than the British, as we may soon find to our cost. On this subject, anyone like myself whose job is interesting though hard must be careful what he says. But when the last grouse against the plumber and his mate has been made, I am bound to say that every time I visit a Works I am impressed with how much men do, not how little—men quite as much as management.

Much of the essential work of the world is not only routine work, some of it is unpleasant. One cannot imagine men offering to do it voluntarily in their leisure. I do not see myself when I retire offering to take on the job of a sewage man as a piece of voluntary work—though perhaps I ought to. In former times the dull unpleasant work was forced upon the political slave and more recently upon the economic slave, and by the white man upon the black man. In totalitarian countries in which a new form of slavery has been introduced, it is forced upon the opponents of the regime and those whom its officials may fear or dislike, and upon prisoners of war. It made one deeply angry to meet boys and girls who had escaped into Western Germany from the mines of Silesia, or prisoners of war and internees who had been released from concentration camps after their body and spirit had been broken by forced labour, and they were no more value to those in control. How should such work be done in a society which is free and Christian? Ought it not in some way to be rationed out? Would it be hurtful if all black-coated workers, including the academic sort, had to do a share in the less agreeable forms of manual work? Might it not do more than all our exhortation to break down class distinctions?[17]

6. *Rest*

I. SUNDAY

As the pattern of society and social habits change, churchmen need to take thought concerning Sunday as

[17] Much is being written on this subject. I would commend especially: Sir George Schuster, *Christianity and Human Factors in Industry* (the Beckly Lectures for 1951); G. Goyder, *The Future of Private Enterprise*; also a joint Pastoral Letter by the Roman hierarchy in the civil Province of Quebec entitled, *The Problem of the Worker*, which summarizes recent Papal Encyclicals.

a day of rest, a subject thoroughly bedevilled by the Lord's Day Observance Society. The fact that the Christian tradition and the Christian values are still deeply embedded in our society is due so much to the way in which Sunday used to be observed that no Christian can see it being transformed into something much more secular than the continental Sunday without anxiety. There are two issues wrapped together. The first is how the Church is to give its witness and do its work of gathering its people for worship and for teaching if the Sunday time-table of society does not allow space for these activities. The other is how to protect the principle of a day of rest in the life of the community from economic pressures such as the extension of the shift system and from the attack of commercialized sport and public amusement, and to do this especially on behalf of the increasing number of people employed in catering and entertainment.[18] On the church side we must recognize and accept the changing pattern of life, and adapt our time-table as far as possible to it. There is nothing sacrosanct about the hours of 8, 11 and 6.30. The Roman Catholics, in France at least, are being more adaptable than Anglicans are. Recently in the Church of S. Germain, beside the Louvre in Paris, I saw a notice of Sunday services on a pillar which gave a list of some twenty churches in the centre of Paris where mass was said and communions made at varying hours between 5.30 and 9.15 on Sunday evenings. In regard to Sunday, we have to do some hard thinking, and be bold to make experiments (and also to call them off), and to have in

[18] e.g. the mining village where on Sundays in summer seventeen charabancs take a hundred or so families to the seaside for a twelve-hour outing; the boy who cannot make his Communion on Sunday because he is delivering milk; the churchwarden who is on shift-work and can only attend one Sunday in three; the employer who lives in a society where cocktail parties at twelve on Sunday are the fashion.

mind not only the needs of the faithful but also the benefit of the whole community.

There is much more to it than just juggling with the hours of Divine Service. Times can safely be adjusted to social custom, but there must also be preparation and discipline. Granted inconvenient timing makes a poor discipline, but discipline there must be. The sad decline in the vigour of Free Church worship seems to have dated from the passing of the Puritan Sabbath, for it left Free Churchmen with no other discipline of worship. It all became too easy among the middle classes. Morning church after a late breakfast; none of the discomfort of kneeling when you got there; apart from hymn-singing, which tended to become more and more sentimental, no vigorous call to participate in a liturgy of the people. Little demand, and so slackening response.

There is an organic connection between discipline (fasting) and prayer. So the Rev. Fr. Perrett, who understands intimately the Liturgical Movement in the French Church, writes of the evening communion in Paris churches and in the homes of the workers where priest-workmen minister.

> 'They are the spearhead and the pattern of the Revival. (Shall I say, they are Paul turned towards the Gentiles? Not quite.) The relaxation of fasting, etc., would be disastrous and would not be tolerated probably, if the Two Missions were not infusing a new spirit, something better into the Church at large. The whole Body is being revivified through great friars and exertions and efforts of great saints; perhaps the time has come slowly to recast the old discipline and standards which have no grip on the New Gentiles.
>
> 'It is how I venture to view the situation. To me, the important things appear to be, not the adoption of such and such practice and method, not such and such

change in outward discipline and time-table, but God's action and the surrender and obedience of his saints.'

Men have to discover that work and worship are the two-fold service man owes to God. In a Christian community the daily work would be the stuff of the Church's liturgy, even as bread and wine—products of men's work—are the elements of the Christian eucharist. They have also to rediscover the recreational value of a rest which is not spiritual sloth. Our society, including the Church and its ministry, is suffering from excessive activism. Too few people are thinking quietly and deeply; scientists and doctors as well as parsons complain that they are all being turned into business and committee men. The prayer life and the necessary activity of the Church are too separate. The only prayer many can get off is the stop-press 'If I forget Thee, do not Thou forget me'. Men cannot tap the limitless spiritual resources of God by hurried ejaculations of that sort, or discover the truth of the saying that 'the looking is what saves us'.

II. WORSHIP AND LIFE

The difficulty which many good people have in relating in their own experience worship and life presents the ordained minister, whose primary function is the conduct of public worship, with a perplexing problem. It is hard for him to comprehend this reluctance and even distaste for public worship. Instead of trying to understand it, he is apt to fall back on admonitions and exhortations, to stress the obligation upon Christians to join in public worship, and to leave it at that. It is, however, futile to leave it at that.[19] Why is it that so

[19] The attempt of the Church Assembly and the Convocations in England, following the lead of the Lambeth Conference in 1948, to lay down rules for the spiritual discipline of the laity, is likely to defeat its laudable intention. It starts off on the wrong foot and

many people whose parents apparently went to church quite happily every Sunday find church services boring? They are bored because what goes forward fails to awaken and hold their attention. It does not speak to their condition in such a way that they are compelled to listen and take part; it does not seem to them to be closely related to their main interests and needs; it does not make much difference—and again one must ask, why? An adequate answer to a problem which is not merely psychological and sociological, but one of faith and belief, cannot be given in a few pages. None the less, something must be said if only to justify the claim already advanced for the keeping of Sunday.

The great theme of the Bible is the union or covenant between God and the People or Church of God. In the mystery of His purpose a small nation was selected to be the people to whose prophets, teachers and faithful ones was revealed the truth about His being, and the saving truth about life. They were chosen not because the Creator of heaven and earth wants courtiers and favourites, but because He requires a body of messengers who will go teach all nations. The story of the Old Testament is largely a tragic story of failure. Eventually, God in His wisdom and mercy manifested Himself in and through Jesus Christ. Out of the old Israel was born the Christian Church, a people of God baptized in the name of Jesus Christ, called to manifest in itself the life of the Holy Trinity and to be the instrument of God's purpose as the Jewish Church had failed to be and do. Every Christian congregation is in its place and time this People of God. The calling of its members, severally

when it ends with six minimum rules for churchmen, it comes down on the side of the good Pharisee in his controversy with Jesus. For Christianity only knows a maximum demand which is a response to the love of God. A weakness of Anglicanism has always been its tendency to water down that commitment and to equate discipleship with conformity.

and together, is to represent Jesus Christ: its common prayer joins with the intercession of Christ for men: its mission is to realize that prayer in the life of the world, persuading men that Jesus is Lord and that grace is given them to be deeply loyal and wholly committed to that faith and life.

The reason why the church community in many a place counts for little and fails to 'advertise the noble acts of God' so as to arouse attention and evoke repentance is that its members have no clear conviction that they are the People of God called to be Christ among men. If they were addressed, in the words of St. Peter, not from the pulpit but in the less devotional surroundings where they expect words to have their face value, 'You are a chosen race, a kingly and priestly house, a people of God's own possession, that you should show forth the praises of Him who has called you out of darkness into His marvellous light', they would not know what to make of it. Their instinctive reply might be 'Not so, we belong to St. Mary's, C. of E. you know, nice church, just raised £500 for electric light—a marvellous improvement.' So long as regular church-goers have no sense of being the People of God, and think of themselves as a collection of individuals who like attending church, inevitably they give the impression that they do not truly know what they are at and why they are at it together. If, on the other hand, churchmen became alive to this truth about themselves and had faith enough to ask God to show them what to do about it and with it, there would be no small stirring of the waters and others might begin to see that worship had some relevance to life.

Nothing less is good enough. For the other side of the picture is that our times, like the early days of the Christian Church, is a day of judgment upon the world and upon the Church, when the foundations are being shaken. In such a time churchmen stand condemned if they are content in their churchmanship to be trivial in their thoughts and actions and turned in upon themselves. Moreover, while churchmen are thus, the demonic powers are not idle. By contrast, the heresy of Communism comes with the force of a gospel to some young people who have a concern for social justice. Like the Gospel, it asks of the individual total commitment, and some give it. The People of God, therefore, are confronted by a two-fold challenge: from God through the Word of God; from men in need of a saving Gospel in a crumbling world. Where companies of Christians are facing this demand, their worship does in fact gain depth and reality, and the House of God becomes a powerhouse in a neighbourhood.

This is the deep level of faith and belief at which the decline of the worshipping habit has to be attacked. There is in addition much else to do.

It is commonly asserted that the 'numinous' instinct around which the practice of worship is built has been destroyed in adults who have been conditioned by an industrial society and by a machine age. These conditions, together with the sensationalism of much propaganda and recreation, have certainly tended to overlay and bury it, so that it has become hard to evoke. It is evoked, however, on occasions and by occasions in the most unlikely people. Who cannot recall acts of worship which have been a deeply moving experience—not in the sense of 'having a good time' emotionally, but because they were apprehended by God and impelled in response to a finer quality of life? 'In thy light we see light.' 'The Kingdom of heaven is at hand; repent.' Sometimes the human situation is the primary fact in evoking this response—a personal sorrow or joy, the sharing with others of a common interest, anxiety and resolve, as in the dark days of 1940 when the people of this country did pray together. These and similar experiences are not to be decried as vestigial Christianity or written down as cupboard love. They are the very stuff of life and the matter of tragedy. Moreover, services when those who assemble are united by a strong attachment—civic, national, vocational—are common worship, and that is why they are appreciated by men who may not be attracted by ordinary church services. Often, too, the prayers at such a service, if it is well ordered, may voice the aspirations and petitions of the congregation and be accompanied by the still silence which betokens close attention. In contrast, it is precisely at this point that the worship in many churches fails, because in practice it is an individual, semi-private affair. If the building is not full, those who come will make it look and feel emptier than it is by sitting as far from one another as they can. This isolationism in the presence of God often reaches its extremity in what some Anglicans call 'the early service'. There one may see a few people scattered about the building, hiding from one another and the priest behind pillars, engaged in their private devotions—as though the Communion was only between several individuals and their God. No greater reform has taken place in the Church of England of late than the renewed emphasis on the corporate nature of worship and of the Holy Communion in particular. Where it has been experienced, both worship and fellowship have been strengthened. For in worship as well as in life, man finds God not only in the vertical relationship—the adoration of the creature for his Creator—but also in the horizontal relationships of man with man. True piety is after the pattern of a triangle, not of a spike. There are no private substitutes for such worship. It is a corporate offering of ourselves with and through Christ to God which brings the will and the power to be fellow-workers with God.

The creative and recreative power of worship, for the rest, resides in the contemplation of perfection and in the fact of God entering in. It is good for men living in an evil world, and conditioned by the secular pressures of a machine age, to look beyond themselves, and also to look up. It is the right kind of escapism, for it should send them back to the ordinary round with 'recruited vigour for the task'. Yes, it is 'the looking that saves us'. The earth is full of the glory of God. If men are not able to see and enjoy that glory here they are not likely to make much of heaven hereafter. It is also good to carry in one's head some beautiful things—melodies, lines of verse, words of Scripture. How impressive is the testimony of men imprisoned in solitary confinement to the steadying effect and comfort of such treasures! It is also wise in these hurrying days to recall the best hours of one's life. Such memories open doors that have become fast. There was a Hebrew poet driven by his surroundings to the verge of despair and unbelief, until he began to recall 'the years of the right hand of the Most High'.

'The universe,' William Temple once said, 'is a divine utterance. It grows more articulate at each stage, and culminates in the Incarnation.' Christian worship as expressed in the liturgy of the Church is man's response to a God who so reveals Himself. And, in fact, men and women will do the daily chores in better heart and fight life's battles more vigorously when the peace of God has come to them in and through the contemplation of His Being and His 'noble acts'. For worship, truly directed and sincerely expressed, is also the coming of God to the worshipper, and that is why it makes men of us. Sacrifice is the point in life where the Spirit of God breaks in with power. In sacrificial worship, when men are identified, unworthy though they be, with the offering of Christ, and their prayers become part of His intercession for mankind, when the praises of the Church on earth mingle with the alleluias of the Church in heaven, the barriers fall away and the love of God enters in. Such worship is finely stretching; an austere joy; a holy and lovely thing. Its moment may pass quickly. To apprehend it while it is present is what matters.

In modern society, one is disposed to think, there is an increase of egoism. This has happened not merely because a competitive society with large prizes for the successful makes men aggressive, or because advertising and propaganda conduce to exhibitionism, but chiefly because humility is often wanting in men who do not look further than their neighbours and acquaintances for their standards of self-criticism. Humility is an invaluable element in society—for it is a quality that makes a man considerate and peaceable and disposes him towards justice and mercy, and without these there cannot be good fellowship. Nevertheless humility is not a virtue but a spiritual grace. It flowers at the foot of the Cross where a man in self-abasement recognizes that he is a debtor to God, and can do no good thing without the power of the Holy Spirit.

This is the point, moreover, where Christianity differs from mysticism. The mystic, in the practice of contemplation, may persuade himself that he can attain perfection and take the Kingdom of heaven by the force of his own mental and spiritual discipline and endeavour. For the Christian, the Cross measures the cost to God of man's redemption and marks the distance between the good man and the Triune God in the beauty of His holiness. And so the Christian sacrament which is after the pattern of what is best in human life recognizes how far short of the goodness of God and how undeserving of His mercy that best is. 'We do not presume to come to this thy table, O merciful Lord, trusting in our own righteousness but in thy manifold and great mercies.'

There rests upon those who conduct public worship the task, not of trying to enforce an obligation, but of stimulating a hunger and thirst, and of providing the means for their satisfaction. Though the root of the trouble, as I have tried to show, lies deeper than all ministerial failures, these in the aggregate are substantial. Those responsible for church services and the care of churches are often poor craftsmen and careless technicians. Ministers, organists, choristers, sidesmen, just do not take sufficient trouble with their respective parts to help people who may only be spiritually half-awake to become fully awake to the living God. They may not be fully awake themselves. We consistently underestimate the amount and the degree of inattention and bad workmanship in so exalted a craft. Too many, after a time, give up trying to improve the quality of what they do. They do not persevere in their own practice of prayer or keep their own thinking fresh and lively.

Moreover, a special effort and much experiment are required in these days to help people, young and old, to pray so that they are able to take part in sustained prayer and to enter fully in the liturgy of the Church. No man in my experience did this better than the late T. W. Pym. With imagination and understanding he began with ordinary men and women where they were. He did not teach them about prayer. He showed them how to pray by doing it with them. Step by step he led them to relate their prayers and their life in such ways as to enlarge and deepen both, and to find in the liturgy of the Church their fulfilment. That is an urgent pastoral and priestly task confronting the ministry of the Church to-day, which requires much patience and sympathetic teaching, and is greatly rewarding.

Let me end this brief discussion of a big subject with two further observations.

The mass of people with no apparent hunger for the things of the spirit, and the smaller group looking for the meaning of life and its expression who think the churches redundant, have to be approached both through the normal ministries and activities of the local church and also outside of them, for the gap is wide and deep. The churches will be most persuasive if they are imbued with the charity of God. Some men and women, however, are called to exert a prophetic and priestly influence in secular groups. In order to do this they may have to work independently of the local churches and often in loneliness. If they were to succumb to the temptation to collect coteries of persons around themselves, they would fail to be ambassadors of Christ or a vanguard of the People of God. A vanguard must be consciously attached to and in communication with the main body. Secondly, churchmen must always remember that as Tillich says, 'the churches are not the whole of our culture'. Those who are maintaining and expressing a creative culture—poets, artists, musicians, scientists, educationalists—are doing an indispensable part of a common task. If the understanding and love of the works of man and the handiwork of God were to fade in whole tracts of society, the ministry of the Church and the preachers of the Cross would be in a poor way. It may even be that the revival of vital religion waits upon the renewal and spread of a creative culture in industrial society.

7. *The Relations of Men and Women*

Lastly, I would single out without attempting to enumerate or discuss them, *all the problems which centre round and in the family* and the relations of men and women. These are by no means problems which have gone by default in our Communion. Indeed, just as in Methodist circles one might be led to think that drink and gambling were the root of all evil, so, among Anglicans, moral welfare is often narrowly interpreted in terms of sex. In regard to the family and marriage, the Church has a principle to uphold, with a wealth of experience behind, and society expects it of us. But there is much more to be done. There is wise guidance to be given and a pastoral ministry to be exercised, and they require both understanding of the changing pattern of society and knowledge of biological and psychological facts as well as of moral principles. Here too we are greatly handicapped by being so middle-class and by our official voices being so clerical and exclusively male.

We all believe that the family is a divine institution and that sound family life is the basis of a sound society. We are all concerned at the number of broken marriages and disrupted families. But it is a quite insufficient answer if we confine ourselves to talking *ad nauseam* about the sanctity of the family and to taking a stiff line about the remarriage of divorced persons. We must do a lot more than that. We have to go further in our analysis and further afield in our remedies for these disorders, and be sure that we are not exalting phases of family life that were far from ideal, such as, for instance, the Victorian paterfamilias, the family as a self-centred and selfish economic unit, or that we are not serving up in a plausible way the old idea of woman as a functional appendage of the male and not a person in her own right.

There is need to give young folk an intelligent conception of human relations and of the place and function of sex in them, including what is called sex instruction; there is need to give to young married couples some wise advice about the difficulties of getting on together, about the inevitable snags and the valuable solvent that a sense of humour and patient good temper provide. At the same time it is wise to recognize a danger in giving advice too readily. The older one gets the more hesitant one is in telling other people how to run their lives. It is better, usually, to help them to unravel the issues objectively, and then leave them to choose their course with such wisdom as God may think fit to give them.

Some of the causes for the break-up of families have nothing to do with sex at all. They are due to social and economic pressures; lack of houses; man and wife both going out to work, and the man perhaps away from home; the failure of some modern legislation to respect the family unit. The removal of these pressures which hinder the good life are to be sought through political action and within industry, and churchmen along with others have to see to it, and not to be content as in past years churchmen were content, to come along with the ambulance when it was too late. I would also throw out in passing that the cure for the excessive emphasis on sex and the crude and constant appeals to the sex instinct in industrial society to-day is not merely to talk still more about it in the name of moral welfare, but to try to widen and enrich the recreations, amusements and interests of the people, so that presently those who make their money by providing amusements and recreations may change the tunes they play and improve their repertoire.

It is important in this sphere to distinguish between the roles of educationalist and practitioner. The Church, through its members, has to play both parts. The educationalist should always be trying to see life whole and to set before people a pattern of life, integrated, rounded, complete—'Be ye perfect even as your Heavenly Father is perfect.' He has to interpret that wholeness of life to men and women as they try to find their way in a disordered society, even as the priest has to help them, sinners though we all are, to worship the Triune God in the fullness of His being and purpose. The practitioner, on the other hand, has to help people to deal with their problems, sicknesses, and sins. He is almost bound to become a little pre-occupied with ill-health and curative methods, even to the extent of becoming rather pathological himself. Consequently, educationalist and practitioner may easily get across one another, unless they learn to respect one another's spheres and functions in the ministry of the Church to men.

It has been good for our Communion that some of its members ministering in its name have learnt from our Lord to take people as they are, and not to put 'keeping standards up' before 'the redemption of persons'. Many moral welfare workers have learnt in the school of experience the humility, the patience, the humour, the love that is not shocked by the sins and follies of men and women, remembering how much we, sinners also, owe to the grace of God, and often to a better chance in life. This pastoral ministry which the trained moral welfare workers exercise is, after all, only a specialized form of a ministry which the whole Church should be exercising. Indeed the specialized ministry becomes frustrated and in vain unless the worshipping community in every neighbourhood is a forgiving society in which fresh starts are possible, its ministry informed and wise, and unafraid of believing in God's power to recreate human lives. An effective ministry of forgiveness leading to repentance can only be exercised within a forgiving society—not outside its door.

V

WHAT SHOULD THE CHURCH BE DOING?

IN every age and place the community of Christians has both to present and also to represent Jesus Christ. Its preachers will only be able to preach the Gospel with persuasive power if the corporate life of the Church is recognizably like the life which they declare to be the Way and the Truth. Its preachers and teachers have both to know the Christian doctrine of God and man and the nature of human society, and also to understand intelligently the contemporary world. They must also 'attend' to the Holy Spirit so as to be open to receive new insights and revelations. At the same time, the men and women who come together with them for worship must continually be trying to fulfil the commandment 'Be ye perfect', without becoming either smug and insincere in their worship, or disheartened and faithless. Success will depend on individual and church life being centred on God in thought and in worship. That means that they have to look out as well as to look up.

They have 'to look out' in two senses. The trouble with those who go often to church, and especially with those who minister in sacred things and say many offices, is that they lose the power of attention. The words run off our backs and out of the door of our minds, geese that we are. We speak the sacred Name and it might be any name; we rattle off the Lord's Prayer and we might just as well say the alphabet. How humbled I was to read the other day:

'Until last September I had never pronounced a liturgical prayer. . . . Since that time I have made a practice of saying it (the Lord's Prayer) through once each morning with *absolute attention.* If during the recitation my attention wanders or goes to sleep in the slightest degree, I begin again until I have once succeeded in going through it with absolutely pure attention. The effect of this practice is extraordinary. At times the very first words tear my thought from my body and transport it to a place outside space where there is neither perspective nor point of view. Filling every part of this infinity of infinity there is silence, a silence which is not an absence of sound, but which is the object of a positive sensation, more positive than that of sound. Sometimes Christ is present with me in person, but his presence is infinitely more real, more moving, more clear than on that first occasion when he took possession of me.'[1]

The other sense in which Christians have to look out is that they have to look outwards and expect to meet the Christ, as von Hügel used to say, not only along the perpendicular line of prayer and worship, but also along the horizontal line of meeting one's fellows, of accepting life's responsibilities, and through an awareness and love of all created things. Moreover, while it is true that human nature does not change, it is also true that we are living in times without precedent. Men's thought of the universe has been stretched far beyond the limits of imagination even if normally they shrink back into their egg shell. The ordinary man has become aware that he is neighbour to other men the world over, and that they are tied together politically, economically, socially, even if normally he withdraws behind parochial bounds. This is asking of them a new way of thought

[1] Simone Weil, *Waiting upon God*, pp. 23-4.

and life related to this new world. Christians are being called to be saints of a new kind—no longer always after the pattern of the medieval cloister. But as yet the Church—not least that part which calls itself catholic—is not so aware of the nature of this new demand as to be a favourable soil for the growth and flowering of a new type of holiness, which will represent the fullness of the Godhead to men whose concept of the universe and of life has been so stretched.

At its best, the membership of the Church is a body of men and women who are responding to the fact of the Cross by accepting the demand of the Cross. It cannot be this truly and fully because it is made up of sinful men and women—many of whom are too complacent about themselves and the sorry state of the institution to be creatively penitent. Unless the whole membership, however, is in some degree conscious of its calling and mission, and unless there is within it a creative minority who have accepted the demand in glad response to what God has done for them, its life is bound to be savourless and lacking in power. On the other hand, the Church on earth cannot escape worldliness, for its members have to live in the world. Its life and economy must in some degree reflect the manners and economics of contemporary society. The issue is, therefore, to what degree. If the Church were wholly other, it could not make contact with secular society. If it becomes too involved and compromised it ceases to be a Church militant. It cannot, as a matter of fact, be completely holy and also catholic at the same time. There has to be a tension in the life of the community as in the life of the individual. When the tension is evaded either by excessive worldliness or by a pietistic or sectarian type of holiness, there is no Cross, no Passion, no Easter joy in its life. In the tension recognized and felt, as well as through the experience of a new sort of holiness, which, as I have just said, it must feel after and find, there will come zest and joy into the Church's life, and the renewal of its spiritual power in the world.

What then must the Church do in order to be a prophetic ministry in contemporary society and speak to men's condition?

One often sees a letter in the press or receives one from a pained or angry or superior-minded correspondent demanding that the Church should say or do something about this or that—world peace, football pools, housing, the atom bomb, blood sports, old age pensions, and the like. These writers always assume that the Church consists of the ordained ministry, and that it should be perfectly possible for an Archbishop or a Pope to make a pronouncement on these subjects on behalf of the whole body. Although that is all that some ask for, others expect the Church to be able by direct action to get things done in the secular world.

While I would not wish to defend the failures of churchmen to exercise a decisive influence for good in the affairs of the world or a nation, I would venture the opinion that there has been no shortage of pronouncements from Archbishops downwards. The ordained ministry talks and protests maybe too much. But any way, bishops, clergy and ministers talking is not the Church acting, for *at least* 999 out of every 1,000 members of the Church are laity.

The failure of the Church to influence and guide the affairs of men, say, in politics and industry, has chiefly been because in its corporate life at all levels there has been so little free discussion, so little exchange of informed opinion, so little attempt corporately to bring Christian insights to bear upon the decisions and personal relationships that make nine-tenths of daily life. The pulpit, and indeed the clergy, can only help up to a point.

A genuine ministry of the Word, spoken by men with an intelligent knowledge of the world in which they are living and with sympathetic intuition of the sort of situations men and women have to meet at home and at work, can help them to bring Christian insights to bear on these situations. If the teaching and the worship are as they should be they can greatly fortify the individual Christian in his daily work and life, and enable him to resist the pressures of mass opinion and be a free thinker—if I may use those words in their true sense. It is not sufficient, however, that first principles should be clearly proclaimed; there has to be a deal more thought given, more intelligence and wisdom directed, to the relating of those principles to the concrete situations that arise in the home, in industry, and in political life.

A man, for example, may know well enough that he ought to 'love his neighbour', but if he belongs to such varied groups as a family, a city, a football club, a nation, a masonic lodge, a Trade Union and a church, he may fairly ask 'And who is my neighbour?', and hope for a little guidance in the matter of priorities. For the most part, a layman is not getting that kind of enlightenment inside his local church, or attempting to give it. I emphasize the giving as well as the getting because it is very much the business of the laity. On them rests the responsibility of making choices and decisions. The concrete situations in a business or industry, moreover, which involve a moral decision as often as not also involve technical and intimate knowledge of that business. The parson who knows his Christian ethics—and not all of us do—is, in regard to that sort of situation, like a spectator of a Rugby football match on the touchline. He may shout at a distant player in the mêlée, 'Lie on the ball, you', but on account of the distance may have failed to see that the ball was no longer there to be lain on. The advice of a fellow-player would be more to the point even though he might be too involved to see the total strategy of the game.

Frankly, I do not think that we are being nearly intelligent enough in our churches about the business—which is everybody's business—of living in a complex and by no means Christian society. We are not doing for one another that sort of elucidating of particular concrete issues which occupies so much of St. Paul's letters. Consequently, churchmen all too often fail to give any lead and just conform to the world, because if your mind is in a mush that is the line of least resistance. Others again of an older generation used to evade the challenge by taking the line—'business is business and religion is religion and I don't let 'em mix'. Because so many laymen and prominent laymen in the churches of last century were allowed to get away with that apostasy, the manual workers were alienated from the churches, and in many European countries Communism has gained the hold which it has. I am not urging that all the laity should become expert theologians. Englishmen dislike theology and Scots are not so fond of theological discussion as they used to be. But these matters and decisions in which Christian insights are needed touch the lives of everybody. They are vital issues of daily life.[2]

As part of *normal* church life there should be more free frank discussion touching the relevance of our faith to life, not just in its more intimate personal aspects, but also in regard to the ministry and influence of the church community in a neighbourhood, and to the part it should play, and with whom it should play, in the life of the community. If a Christian congregation is

[2] As one example of what I have in mind, I would point to the absence of guidance for those who have to act in a representative capacity. How far, and in what circumstances, should someone in such a position act as he would act if he had only himself to consider and could freely do what was right in his own eyes?

at sufficient depth a fellowship in Christ, it should be able to carry within it differences of opinion and judgment, and be the stronger in its unity on that account. The parish meeting, which is partly what I have in mind, is one of the valuable revivals in the churches of our communion at the present time, tying in as it should with the parish communion. It can follow many patterns, but what it should never be is a class where the priest pretends to be the oracle which he is not. It should be a meeting of laity about real issues and concerns, in which they try to grow a common mind—the priest rather deliberately sitting back, using the rudder sparingly, putting in a word when a relevant principle or a doctrine is being overlooked.

Unless during the next half century churchmen are more intelligent about Christian morality and life, they are going to 'sell out' to Communism. For Communism is attracting many young people as the churches are not, and it is appealing not just to their cupidity or to their excessive faith in technology, but to their readiness to venture much in response to a demand on their total loyalty. It is also providing them with an explicit and realizable programme of action. Therefore Marxist Communism will not be overcome by brute force or by intelligent argument alone. Those who see its falsity and know the full horror of the attempt to put it into operation will have not only to out-think its exponents but also to out-live them. More than twenty years ago W. R. Inge wrote with prescience: 'No religion can satisfy the needs of our time which does not both understand secular aspirations and transcend them. . . . We seem to be in the last phase of a long movement of emancipation which divides the modern period from the medieval.' 'The temper which runs into any port in a storm will not be the prevailing temper of the twentieth century, unless indeed (as I do not expect) the Red International terrifies Europe into throwing itself into the arms of the Black.'[3]

In conclusion, the kind of corporate thinking within the Fellowship for which I have been pleading has also to be extended to those who are of the Christian frontier and beyond. In society to-day men and women in various professions are now doing the work and exercising the influence which as late as the sixteenth century was being done and exercised by the ordained ministry of the Church. To-day the successors of the medieval clergy, who, being the only men in society with some education, had to do many things, are not only the ordained ministry but also professors and teachers, social workers, personnel managers, doctors and journalists. This composite band, as Br. Every, S.S.M., pointed out in an article in *The Guardian,* carrying further an idea of S. T. Coleridge over a hundred years ago, is the modern clerisy. They are the guardians and the transmitters of that Christian culture which is our British inheritance. Those who in various ways guide the community in its thought should see themselves and others in the character of a modern clerisy, and should come together to share their experience and wisdom; and in this co-operation the ordained ministry of the Church have their part. This deliberate coming together would have the additional merit of countering the strong tendency to specialization and intellectual isolationism between the several departments of knowledge which the extension of knowledge and functional pressures are causing. One's hope would be that those who would thus come together—the clerisy of our time—would discover themselves to be, if not practising churchmen, at least what T. S. Eliot has called the Community of Christians.

[3] W. R. Inge, *Christian Ethics and Modern Problems.*

Quite deliberately I have not discussed directly world politics and international relations. This omission is not due to unawareness that a third world war might destroy, as the second world war has so nearly destroyed, western culture and civilization, which are more Christian than they are anything else, for nearly all that is good in them stems from Christianity. It would be sectarian folly if the Church in its task of leading men into eternal life ceased to care for the civilization which has become the soil, the climate, the very air in which it grows and lives, or for the culture which it has inspired.[4]

The enemy, however, which Christianity has to overcome in the second half of the twentieth century is not confined behind the iron curtain that divides Europe. It is not exclusively 'the surgeons of the Kremlin' or even Marxist Communism, it is the new secularism of a technological age and an industrial society which is impatient and careless of persons and human values, and thinks and plans in terms of categories and graphs on the assumption that man was made for the machine. This new secularism is pervading the whole world—America as well as Russia. Its threat to mankind will not pass when the threat of Marxist Communism passes or when Russian imperialism is contained or when the rising nationalism of the East and in Africa settles comfortably into the pattern of a world community. The only sufficient answer to the threat of a scientism which would dispense with a Father in heaven and deliver us into the efficient hands of planners and omnicompetent rulers is the Christian faith, once delivered, newly interpreted, obediently realized in action and life by men and women moved by the compulsion of Divine Love. 'Only Perfection is sufficient.'

[4] Cf. my own lectures on *Church Strategy in a Changing World*, Hodder & Stoughton, 1950.

VI

ETERNAL LIFE

In the Alpine valley where I am writing, such is the formation of rock that a mountain torrent will disappear into the earth, and after flowing underground for some way will rise again to the surface and rush along with added exuberance. The phrase, the Kingdom of God, and the thought which it holds, have followed a similar course down the centuries. After a long seclusion they rose in the nineteenth century to the conscious surface of religious thought, and in my time the phrase has been stretched to cover the whole of man's life as touched by faith and is used with careless frequency.

It is noteworthy that the earliest and greatest exponents of the Christian faith were aware of its inadequacy and were, perhaps unconsciously, driven to employ other language. Strictly speaking, the phrase belongs to the vocabulary of politics rather than to that of devotion. The Kingdom of God was a political ideal among the Jews—a state of society where the will of God is sovereign. Our Lord used it in this sense while He tried to give the Jews a different idea of the character of that sovereignty. It was understood in this sense by the Apostles. Both St. John and St. Paul, however, found, as we must surely find, that the language of citizenship is cold metaphor in which to describe the intimate relationship of the human soul with God. True, our Lord once at least did use the expression in that way, but the occasion justified the use. It was to men who were inquiring the precise situation of the Kingdom in time and space, and perhaps were perplexed, as men in recent years have been perplexed, by those who went about crying, Lo here, Lo there, that He replied, the Kingdom of God is within you. The answer perfectly served its purpose. But the expression is as awkward as the paradox is bold.

In the Epistles and in the Fourth Gospel, as one might expect, the language of personal religion is richer than in the Synoptics. St. Paul gives us great words like regeneration, salvation, and speaks of 'life in Christ'; St. John more simply of 'life', 'eternal life'. Undoubtedly the individualistic trend in Christianity owes a good deal to the changes and additions they made in the language of the faith. But we shall not do justly by the Pauline conception of 'salvation' or the Johannine 'eternal life' until we perceive that they approximate to the Synoptic 'Kingdom of God'; and, conversely, our interpretation of 'Kingdom of God' will remain political and external, if not secular and unspiritual, unless we perceive that the life of the Kingdom is of the quality which St. John calls 'eternal', and that the citizen of the Kingdom is the man who is 'regenerate' and knows in himself the experience of 'salvation'. One of the most fruitful discoveries which can be made by anyone who is beginning to study the New Testament is that under different terms the Synoptic, Johannine, and Pauline groups of writings are trying to describe substantially the same thing. Eternal life is the life of the Kingdom, the life of God in which men may in degree share. The advantage of St. John's paraphrase—if it was his and not our Lord's—is that it does not so readily lead to the kind of thought contained in the question put to our Lord—a way of thinking which the phrase 'the Kingdom of God' provokes among men to-day as much as among men whose background was Jewish. 'The Kingdom of God' is not nearly so intelligible an expression as some preachers assume. Even when a man reads, 'My kingdom is not of this world', he is apt to picture another world in the same style as this one for the Kingdom to be in.[1]

In this essay I wish to limit myself to three questions. What does 'having eternal life' here and now, mean? How can we have this life, this Kingdom within ourselves? What should be the relation between it and the conception of a God-directed social order, visible here upon earth?

I

'Be not anxious for your life what ye shall eat or for your body what ye shall put on. . . . Seek ye first the Kingdom of God, and these things shall be added unto you.' This passage which we like to read and hear read for the music of its words, but which we rarely have the courage to believe, follows a stern warning against covetousness—a man's life consisteth not in the abundance of things which he possesses—and an ironical picture of a man who is absorbed in the development of big business up to the night of his death. A man's true life does not consist in bank-notes, furniture, clothes, food and drink, gossip or ecclesiastical routine. The man who is absorbed in these things, far from possessing the Kingdom, does not even see it.

In what, then, does a man's true life consist? There are in the lives of all men hints and veiled intimations of the right answer—experiences on another plane to that on which they usually live. There is human affection, for example. The sight and touch of someone we

[1] It is therefore not a little strange that those who insist that we must express our theology in the language of the plain man should use the expression so freely.

love may excite our love, but love will often continue and even grow stronger where there is no visible contact. It is independent of circumstance. It cannot be bought or sold; its value is in itself. The storms of life break against it, but they cannot break it. Not even death can destroy it. The *Divine Comedy, King Lear, Lycidas, Adonais, In Memoriam,* like David's Lament for Jonathan and Saul, express the common experience of mankind, that human love in its highest range is indestructible, eternal.

Or again, a man hears or sees a masterpiece of art. He says it is beautiful. He does not mean that it is very expensive or useful, but simply that it has a quality which gives him joy and satisfaction. It is an end in itself, one of the absolutes of life. Many years ago I heard the twenty-third Psalm being sung by the choir of the Temple Church. In the singing, music and words fitted so perfectly that one had to smile—it was utterly satisfying. None of the meaningless chanting which one has often heard since can destroy the reality of that experience. Or there come times when a man is drawn out of himself by the intense and exquisite loveliness of flowers or the austere majesty of a range of ice-bound mountains. In that moment he is both humbled and made glad. No price can be put upon these things, no use can be made of them, but he rejoices that they are there; he knows their value is beyond price, and he feels that the greater his power to enter into their beauty and purity, the more truly he is alive. St. Paul once said of a good action, 'No one shall rob me of this crown of glorying'; the expression is also appropriate to an experience of nature's beauty and grandeur.

Experiences, relationships and actions of this kind in the ordinary life of men give a clue to what our Lord meant by 'life' and 'having the Kingdom within' oneself. As Clutton Brock so admirably showed in *What is the Kingdom of Heaven* and elsewhere, the Kingdom of Heaven meant for Jesus Reality. To know that truth, beauty, goodness, love are the supremely valuable things in life and to search them out, is to seek first the Kingdom; to love them and to make them is to have the Kingdom within. It is to allow the mind to dwell on those things in life which are true, honourable, just, lovely, and of good report and not merely to think about them, but to follow thought with action, and *do* them. The Kingdom is not far distant from the man who values life in this way. It will be a joy set before him which will enable him to endure mockery and persecution at the hands of those who do not see.

It is at this point that organized Christianity falls short of the stature of Christ. It often refuses to recognize that our fellowship in Christ must be narrow and incomplete until we believe that the value He attached to things are the true values and try to act on the belief. The religion of Christ is commensurate with life itself—that is its glory; but that of many Christians is immeasurably smaller. Their religion contains no suggestion of the length, depth and height of the glory of God as they are reflected in His creation. And that is why many who have felt the spaciousness of life and have a strong sense of community with people and groups outside the Church feel, when they are asked to join a church, that they are being asked to go from the open air into a small parlour where the blinds are always half-drawn and the windows have not been opened for a long time.[2]

'Reality' and 'absolute values' are, none the less, cold synonyms for the warm and vivid thought of the Gospels. If they are accepted as sufficient there is danger that an

[2] Cf. Simone Weil's reasons for not seeking Baptism in *Waiting upon God*, pp. 4-6.

essential element in our Lord's teaching about the Kingdom may be left out—namely, communion with God—Love. It is important to say this explicitly, because many people to-day are unwilling to see that love and goodness have not an independent existence as abstract forces and are only predicable of personality. According to the New Testament, what gives warmth, colour and life to reality is the fact of God, the possibility of intercourse and friendship between the human son and the heavenly Father. When our Lord speaks of this the imagery of the Kingdom falls away and the more intimate picture of the family takes its place. The Kingdom is the blessed will of a heavenly Father and a fellowship of those who know themselves to be His sons and daughters. 'This is eternal life, to know the Father, the only real God, and Jesus Christ whom He has sent.'

The man who recognizes that truth as the scientist seeks it, beauty as the artist finds it, goodness and love as they exist in human life are corner-stones of the Kingdom, is not far from that Kingdom; but it is the man who knows and loves Him from whom they have their origin and rejoices humbly in the mercy of God, who indeed 'has the Kingdom within'.

II

Jesus told Nicodemus that unless he were 're-born' he would not even see the Kingdom of God. Whether the remark was meant for all men may be questioned. It is certainly true of people as far on in life as Nicodemus probably was. But it is less true of youth. Before the need of forgiveness and renewal can be felt there needs to come a vision of the Kingdom, if it be only a glimpse through the clouds, such as Paracelsus had of a distant city upon a hill:

. . . when suddenly its spires afar
Flashed through the circling clouds; you may conceive
My transport. Soon the vapours closed again,
But I had seen the city, and one such glance
No darkness could obscure. . . .[3]

It is from an initial glimpse of the purpose of God that there comes the sense of unfitness and unworthiness which is the only fruitful sense of sin. The Church fails when it calls on men to repent without showing them the Kingdom which is at hand, for only such a vision is likely to convince them that it is worth while to give up opinions and ways which otherwise might seem good enough. To preach duty and self-denial at youth and not to set before him first of all the vision which will justify the discipline and sacrifice is a failure in psychological insight. It is an inversion of the 'good news' as enunciated by Jesus Himself—The Kingdom is at hand: repent. So in our time before preaching can move men to repentance it must be able to set before them a vision of God's Kingdom, which will quicken imagination and evoke a strong response.

It will be equally disastrous, however, if we assume, as there is a tendency to assume, that it is only necessary to set forth the superhuman attractiveness of the Jesus of history and of the Kingdom of God in order to convert men to its service and His. Psychology and history make nonsense of the assumption. The Jesus of history attracted crowds; but He only held a handful. Men were not ready to pay the price in self-conquest and sacrifice which would make His Kingdom a reality upon earth and in themselves. And the last thing Jesus ever allowed His followers to imagine was that He was providing them with a short-cut to Zion. Count the cost,

[3] Robert Browning: *Paracelsus.*

He said. Having set before them the vision of the Kingdom, He bade them follow Him, and showed them that the way to the Kingdom led through the Cross. There is no other way.

Baron von Hügel has likened Christianity to an ellipse with two foci; there is the fullness of life and its joy, and there is discipline, conflict, and the Cross; green pastures, and the wilderness. But it is always the one way which leads across stony and dangerous places and now through laughing valleys. The two elements in Christianity are wedded together as closely as sunshine and shadow. Strength comes through the recognition of our inability to save ourselves, freedom through the acceptance of responsibility, through sacrifice. A going-out into the wilderness where man learns to distinguish the things of the Spirit; at times, and for some all the time, a rigorous asceticism—these are the conditions of re-birth into fuller life. Only so can man 'harness his fiery energies to the service of light', and become a supple instrument of the Spirit of God, strong, single in mind and heart, and happy.

There is a cryptic sentence in St. Mark, attenuated in St. Luke and altered in St. Matthew, which in a picturesque way states the two-fold nature of the Christian life.

> 'There is no man that hath left house, or brethren, or sisters, or mother, or father, or children, or lands, for my sake and for the Gospel's sake, but he shall receive a hundredfold now in this present time, houses and brethren and sisters, and mothers and children, and lands, with persecutions; and in the world to come eternal life.' (St. Mark 10.29-30.)

Intent upon God and devoted to the service of the Kingdom, the soul is prepared to give up, and does give up everything—the good along with the bad in the relationships of life. It goes out into the wilderness. It dies. But unlike asceticism, Christianity does not end in the wilderness. The soul is re-born there and comes back into the world filled with the grace of God, and, coming back, it finds that the old relationships have gained infinitely in meaning. They are 'received back', multiplied a hundredfold in quality—the clumsy repetition is surely deliberate. The soul that was dead is alive again; and it was only through dying that it has been made fit to 'receive the Kingdom' and enjoy the fellowship of the risen Christ.

There is much in life to throw light on the words. A woman loves her family in a narrow and possessive way which makes her indifferent to the larger claims of humanity. Some catastrophe like a war forces these larger claims upon her. She yields to them; she makes the sacrifice willingly; she begins to care for other families than her own. Does she love her own less? Surely not. Her love for them gains infinitely—a hundredfold—in quality. Or there is a familiar landscape which we have passed daily without thinking it worth notice until one evening we see it transfigured—so it seems—in the light of a setting sun and we begin to find in it a beauty we never knew was there. A man has a happy home, but towards the end of July he is tired, and it bores him. Then he has a good holiday and comes back feeling 'a different man'. When he enters his house it seems a hundred times more attractive than before, and he exclaims: 'How jolly it is to be back—after all, there's no place like home!' The lover in the first full rapture of that experience cries out:

. . . I who thought to sink
Was caught up into love and taught the whole
Of life in a new rhythm.

The lesser conversions of life help towards an understanding of the conversion which our Lord described as re-birth, so completely does it raise a man to another level of being and change his whole outlook. It is the old life lived in a new way. The same notes but a new rhythm and a richer tone. As George Fox said, 'Creation gives out another smell than before'. The moment of awakening when the Kingdom comes to a man none can foretell, but it does not come until he has humbled himself before the Cross, and has repented from the values of the world to those of the Sermon on the Mount and the Life which perfectly embodied its teaching. 'He that hath the Son hath the life'; and the life is not man's achievement but the gift of God.

My song is love unknown,
My Saviour's love to me,
Love to the loveless shown,
That they might lovely be.
O who am I,
That for my sake,
My Lord should take
Frail flesh, and die?

Here might I stay, and sing.
No story so divine;
Never was love, dear King,
Never was grief like thine.
This is my Friend,
In whose sweet praise
I all my days
Could gladly spend.[4]

[4] Samuel Crossman, 1624-83.

III

The final question remains. It is the hardest to answer, and the answer comes indirectly. In the second part of the saying already quoted from St. Mark's Gospel there are two significant words. The disciple who has given up all will receive back the things and relationships which he has renounced multiplied 'a hundredfold now in this present time', but 'with persecutions'. Here in this present life joy will be his, but no fullness of joy; the life of God will refresh his spirit, but the fellowship will be incomplete because he is earth-bound, and often it will be broken by his own sin and the sin of the world. And not only sin, but also his power to love will persecute his joy. The salvation of the individual tarries upon the salvation of society, and the authentic Christian is willing that it should be so. While the mystic with 'naked intent upon God' pursues heaven the Christian will ever and again look back upon the world and refuse to be content in a joy that he cannot share with his fellows.[5]

Indeed if he follows the pattern set on the Mount there may come moments when to help a brother he may allow clouds to hide God from his sight. 'Lord, Thou knowest how busy I must be this day—if I forget Thee, do not Thou forget me.' And God does not forget. If the business is according to His will the prayer will be abundantly answered. The sacrificial principle, he that loses his life finds it, holds right through life—even here in its highest reaches. The mystic's desire is to find God and meet Him, as it were, face to face; the Christian is content to be found of God doing His will. God is not always where He is sought and often He comes to men

[5] Cf. St. Paul: 'To depart and be with Christ . . . is very far better; and yet to abide in the flesh is more needful for your sake.' Phil. 1.23-4.

unawares and assumes unlikely forms—'When saw we thee hungry and in prison. . .' It is a fallacy due to an excessive emphasis on 'experience' that the soul is only in God's presence and being filled by His Spirit when it thinks or feels that it is. The man who lives fully in the world will be found of God and come to know Him in ways undiscovered by those who only search the heavens for Him.

In her admirable book upon the *Life of the Spirit*, the late Evelyn Underhill quoted a fine saying from Boehme as a rebuke of the restlessness of modern Christianity: 'Heaven is just the manifestation of the Eternal One wherein everyone worketh and willeth in quiet love.' The rebuke is timely, because some are trying to fashion the Kingdom on earth with the stuff of this world's life and forget that the Kingdom comes from above. We are often so busy in good works that we have no leisure to rest in the Lord, and in consequence we renew neither our own strength nor that of others.

Nevertheless it is just at this point that we find the difference between the mystical and the specifically Christian experience. While the world suffers the Christian must suffer with it. His desire is not only to taste the joys of heaven, but also to redeem the world. In this life the beatitude of quiet love, however much he may yearn for it, cannot be wholly his—just as it was not Christ's in Gethsemane. As he enters fully into the sufferings of Christ and identifies himself with the need of humanity, its sin will cloud for him the heavenly vision and its cries will ever and again drown the angels' song.

The two avenues of approach are complementary. 'The Christian life,' says Baron von Hügel in a characteristically well-packed sentence, 'must and shall exhibit contact with and renunciation of the Particular and Fleeting; and with this ever seeks and finds the Eternal—

deepening and incorporating within its own experience this "Transcendent Otherness".' It is surely a failure to qualify her mysticism which made Evelyn Underhill argue that 'to seek the Eternal' really covers the first clause. The natural as well as the supernatural is God's sphere. He is to be found in the Particular and Fleeting. It is contact with the Particular and Fleeting—and there must be contact before renunciation can be real—and belief in the abiding value of such contacts, which give richness and fullness to the Christian life; and it is the partial absence of that contact and a disbelief in its abiding value which makes much evangelicalism an attenuated version of the Gospel and the literature of mysticism so monochrome and tedious.

In the Christian mystics there is sometimes uncertainty as to the *differentia* between their creed and that of mystics of another faith, and a tacit avowal that the mystic fraternity is a higher order and a closer bond than a common Christianity. The mystic is liable to be preoccupied with his experience; the Christian is preoccupied not with the processes of faith, but with its object. The 'uniqueness of Christianity' resides in the belief that 'God was *in Christ* reconciling the world to Himself' and in its firm root, in history.[6] 'Again and again,' wrote Evelyn Underhill, 'it has been proved that those who aim at God do better work than those who start with the declared intention of benefiting their fellow-men.' It depends entirely on the God at which they aim. It is true within the circle of Christianity, but it is not always true within the wider circle of theism. It is true within Christianity, for the specifically Christian

[6] 'If history be not the revelation of God, Jesus' striving becomes incomprehensible. If you admit Christ you admit history. Christ's connection with history appears most clearly from His waiting for the immediate decisive breaking in of God's realized Kingdom.' Söderblom, *The Living God*, p. 369.

experience and knowledge of God is in and through Christ.

The mystic, moreover, is inclined in discussion and sometimes in life to distinguish between spiritual religion and (mere) morality; to the Christian the distinction is highly abstract and remote from reality. His religion is one which is 'intrinsically and overwhelmingly moral', so that a certain way of life follows, naturally and inevitably. The Spirit whom he invites to guide his life is a moral being, the same Spirit who dwelt in Jesus of Nazareth. Fellowship with God is always a moral relationship of a distinctive character—in Christ—and leads to a distinctive way of life—the Kingdom of God. That is why the least in the Kingdom of God is greater than the most advanced of, say, Sufi saints.

This attempt to distinguish Christianity from mystical and 'evangelical' interpretations of the Faith is made necessary because only when the distinction is recognized does the relation between the conception of the Kingdom as immanent and the conception of the Kingdom as political become clear. The two conceptions come together in the Christian doctrine of God. God is love. 'Everyone that loveth is begotten of God and (through loving) knows God.' As men grow in the knowledge of God in Christ they begin to understand the true nature of love—love whose expression is both justice and peace, joy and anger. If a man loves God in Christ he must love his fellows at the same time. The Golden Rule is not two separate commandments but one—the single response of the soul to reality. The test of the visions and experiences of the soul is, 'What fruits dost thou bring back from thy vision?'[7] If the Kingdom of God is within it will work itself out in service and fellowship, in thought and action. For love is primarily a principle of

[7] Jacopone da Todi is said to have tested his pupils in mysticism with this question.

action; and can only be expressed in action and in words which have the quality of action, words which are, like Luther's, 'half-battles'.

Moreover, since God is love the life of God among men is manifested in a society. The individual can neither keep it to himself nor possess it fully by himself. When he is tempted to be satisfied with the contemplation of the Divine Goodness he will remember the emphasis of Christ upon *doing* the will of God—'Go thou and do likewise.'[8] The experience of the Kingship of love within his soul will drive him out to share it with all men—that will be his cross and his joy.

An individual faith, however choice, which ignores the fact that we are 'members one of another' and does not express itself in action is less than Christian; while a political Christianity which is merely political is futile. Only those who by discipline, by attentive prayer and in humility of spirit make ready to receive the life of the Kingdom are able to work together with God in the realizing, in the here and now community, of that Kingdom which has its perfect fruition beyond history in eternity.

[8] It comes as a revelation to discover how often, according to St. Luke, our Lord in His teaching uses the verb, to do, or an equivalent phrase.

person, and can only be expressed in action and in words which have the quality of action, words which are like Luther's, "half battles."

Moreover, since God is love, the life of God among men is manifested in a person. The individual can neither grasp nor attain nor possess it fully by himself. When he is tempted to be satisfied with the contemplation of the Divine goodness he must remember the emphasis of Christ upon doing the will of God: "Go thou and do likewise."[1] The experience of the Kingship of love within his soul will drive him out to share it with others—else will he miss love and his joy.

An individual faith or love, an attitude which ignores the fact that we are members one of another, and does not express itself in a society is not Christian. Only a [illegible] of Christianity which is merely personal is half. Only those who by discipline in [illegible] and in [illegible] make ready to receive the life of the Kingdom may also be workers together with God in the realizing, in the here and now, [illegible] community of that Kingdom which has its perfect fruition beyond history in eternity.

[1] It comes as a revelation to discover how often, according to St. Luke, our Lord in His teaching used the verb to do, or an equivalent phrase.

BIBLIOGRAPHY

BARRY, Bishop F. R., *The Relevance of Christianity.* Nisbet.

NIEBUHR, Reinhold, *The Nature and Destiny of Man.* Nisbet.

ELIOT, T. S., *The Idea of a Christian Society.* Faber.

BAILLIE, John, *The Belief in Progress.* O. U. Press.

BARKER, C. J., *The Way of Life.* Lutterworth Press.

LINDSAY, A. D., *The Two Moralities.* Eyre & Spottiswoode.

TEMPLE, Archbishop W., *Citizen and Churchman.* Eyre & Spottiswoode.

INGE, W. R., *Christian Ethics and Modern Problems.* Hodder & Stoughton.

RUSSELL, Bertrand, *Power: A Social Analysis.* Allen & Unwin.

GARBETT, Archbishop C., *In an Age of Revolution.* Hodder & Stoughton.

SCHUSTER, G., *Christianity and Human Relations in Industry.* Epworth Press.

ROBERTS, Michael, *The Estate of Man.* Faber.

WEIL, Simone, *Waiting upon God.* Faber.

OLDHAM, J. H., *Work in Modern Society.* S.C.M. Press.

HARRISON, D. E. W., *Christian Ethics and the Gospel.* Lutterworth Press.

RADCLIFFE, Lord, *The Problem of Power.* Secker & Warburg.

INDEX